The Normative and Regulatory Challenges for the Implementation of the European Deforestation-Free Regulation in Third Affected Countries

Paula Wojcikiewicz Almeida ·
Gabriel Ralile de Figueiredo Magalhães ·
Lucas da Cunha Vollers · Vitor Furtado de Melo

The Normative and Regulatory Challenges for the Implementation of the European Deforestation-Free Regulation in Third Affected Countries

A Brazilian Case-Study

Springer

Paula Wojcikiewicz Almeida
FGV Centre for Global Law and Jean Monnet Centre of Excellence
Getulio Vargas Foundation (FGV)
Rio de Janeiro, Brazil

Gabriel Ralile de Figueiredo Magalhães
FGV Centre for Global Law and Jean Monnet Centre of Excellence
Getulio Vargas Foundation (FGV)
Rio de Janeiro, Brazil

Lucas da Cunha Vollers
FGV Centre for Global Law and Jean Monnet Centre of Excellence
Getulio Vargas Foundation (FGV)
Rio de Janeiro, Brazil

Vitor Furtado de Melo
FGV Centre for Global Law and Jean Monnet Centre of Excellence
Getulio Vargas Foundation (FGV)
Rio de Janeiro, Brazil

ISBN 978-3-032-08457-6 ISBN 978-3-032-08458-3 (eBook)
https://doi.org/10.1007/978-3-032-08458-3

This Springer imprint is published by the registered company Springer Nature Switzerland AG
The registered company address is: Gewerbestrasse 11, 6330 Cham, Switzerland

Acknowledgements The authors would like to extend their gratitude to current and former researchers of FGV Rio Law's Centre for Global Law and the Jean Monnet Centre of Excellence on EU-LA Global Challenges (2023–2026), co-funded by the European Union, for their valuable help in conducting research and in discussing preliminary versions of this text. Particularly, we would like to thank researchers Natália Barcelos, Livia Lamour, Ana Carolina Vasconcelos and Pedro Ortman for their invaluable collaborations for the final product. All figures and tables featured in the book and the appendix were developed by the authors. Unauthorised reproduction without proper credit is disallowed.

Co-funded by
the European Union

Views and opinions expressed are however those of the author(s) only and do not necessarily reflect those of the European Union or the European Education and Culture Executive Agency (EACEA). Neither the European Union nor EACEA can be held responsible for them.

Competing Interests The authors have no competing interests to declare that are relevant to the content of this manuscript.

About This Book

This book analyses the normative and regulatory challenges related to the indirect implementation of the European Deforestation-Free Regulation (EUDR) in Brazil. As part of a broader plan of action to tackle deforestation and forest degradation globally, the EUDR (Regulation (EU) 2023/1115) is a demand-side measure aimed at mitigating greenhouse gas emissions and biodiversity loss through the regulation of relevant commodity trade within the European Union (EU).

Some producing countries, however, are concerned that the EUDR will affect their production chains and generate high costs to comply with it. Although the EUDR does not directly apply to other countries (third countries) normative framework, its potential extraterritorial effects require them to comply with the regulation to be able to introduce their products into the EU's market, thus categorizing an 'indirect implementation'. In this context, Brazil, as a major producer and dependent on the export of its commodities, is very sensitive to how this issue may affect its economy.

This book seeks to address what are the normative and regulatory challenges policymakers and economic players face when indirectly implementing the EUDR in Brazil. To this end, this work analyses how public and private actors interact within Brazil's normative and regulatory framework in light of the EUDR.

The book innovates the discussion both in Brazil and under the international law. Firstly, it brings a systematic methodology. The research employs a mixed methodological approach, comprising theoretical and empirical analysis in order to address the EUDR's normative and regulatory challenges in Brazil. Secondly, the book critically assesses the potential effects and challenges of the EUDR, taking into account the existence of contrasting national implementation mechanisms, such as monitoring, traceability and certification tools.

The results found in this book can bolster suggestions and alternatives to strategies related to the EUDR's adaptation process. In addition, it can promote sustainable practices and improve forest-related framework in third countries, particularly in Brazil.

Contents

About the Authors

Paula Wojcikiewicz Almeida, Professor of International Law and EU Law at FGV Rio Law (since 2008). Director of the Jean Monnet Centre of Excellence on EU-LA Global Challenges, co-funded by the European Commission, at the FGV Rio Law. Director of the Centre for Global Law at the FGV Rio Law. Associate Researcher at the Institute of International and European Law at the Sorbonne (IREDIES). Qualified as 'maître des conferences' in Public Law (France, CNU). Chair of the Interest Group on 'International Courts and Tribunals' of the Latin American Society of International Law (LASIL). Doctorate with honours summa cum laude in International and European Law at the Université Paris 1 Panthéon-Sorbonne. Masters of Law (Master II Recherche—former DEA) in Public International and European Law—Université Paris XI, Faculté Jean Monnet. Postdoctoral visiting scholar at the Max Planck Institute for Comparative Public Law and International Law (2014). Visiting professor at the École de droit de la Sorbonne, Université Paris 1 Panthéon-Sorbonne (2019 and 2024). Visiting professor at the University of Salzburg (since 2017). Visiting professor at the International Studies Programme of the Universidade Católica Portuguesa no Porto (since 2023). Director of Studies at the French-speaking session of the Winter Courses of The Hague Academy of International Law (2024).

Gabriel Ralile de Figueiredo Magalhães, Researcher at the FGV Rio Law's Jean Monnet Centre of Excellence on EU-LA Global Challenges, co-funded by the European Commission, and the Centre for Global Law. PhD student in Regulatory Law at FGV Rio Law. MSc in Maritime Studies at the Naval War College (EGN). He holds an MBA/E in Foreign Trade from the Federal University of Rio de Janeiro (UFRJ), a LL.B. in Law from the Federal University of the State of Rio de Janeiro (UNIRIO), and a BA in International Relations from the Pontifical Catholic University of Rio de Janeiro (PUC-Rio).

Lucas da Cunha Vollers, Researcher at FGV Rio Law's Jean Monnet Centre of Excellence on EU-LA Global Challenges, co-funded by the European Commission, and the Centre for Global Law. Master in International Law from the State University of Rio de Janeiro (UERJ). LL.B. in Law from the Pontifical Catholic University of Rio de Janeiro (PUC-Rio).

Vitor Furtado de Melo, Researcher at FGV Rio Law's Jean Monnet Centre of Excellence on EU-LA Global Challenges, co-funded by the European Commission, and the Centre for Global Law. Master in Political Science (UNIRIO), Msc candidate in Social Anthropology (MN/UFRJ), and LL.B. in Law (UNIRIO).

Abbreviations

APP	Permanent Preservation Areas
CAR	Rural Environmental Registry
CISG	Convention on Contracts for the International Sale of Goods
CONAB	National Supply Company
CONAMA	National Council for the Environment
CONAREDD+	National REDD+ Committee
CSDDD	Corporate Sustainability Due Diligence Directive
CTE	Committee on Trade and Environment
DDS	Due Diligence Statement
DETER	Deforestation Detection System in Real Time
DSB	Dispute Settlement Body
DSU	Dispute Settlement Understanding
EM	Equivalence Mechanism
EU	European Union
EUDR	European Deforestation-Free Regulation
EUTR	European Union Timber Regulation
FAQ	Frequently Asked Questions
FLEGT	Forest Law Enforcement, Governance and Trade Action Plan
FNDF	National Fund for Forestry Development
GATT	General Agreement on Tariffs and Trade
GCP	Global Coffee Platform
GHG	Greenhouse Gases
GTA	Animal Transit Guide
IBAMA	Brazilian Institute of the Environment and of Renewable Natural Resources
ICMBio	Institute Chico Mendes of Conservation and Biodiversity
IEF	State Forestry Institute
INDE	National Spatial Data Infrastructure
IS	Information System
ITC	International Trade Centre
LINDB	Introductory Law to the Norms of Brazilian Law

MAPA	Ministry of Agriculture, Livestock and Food Supply
MMA	Ministry of the Environment and Climate Change
MMU	Minimum Mapping Unity
MPIA	Multi-Party Appeal Arbitration Arrangement
NGO	Non-Governmental organization
PIL	Private International Law
PMABB	Environmental Monitoring Program for Brazilian Biomes
PPCDAM	Action Plan for the Prevention and Control of Deforestation in the Legal Amazon
PPCerrado	Cerrado Action Plan
PPM	Process and Production Methods
PRODES	Legal Amazon Satellite Project
RL	Legal Reserve
SEAPA	Secretariat of Agriculture, Supply and Livestock
SEMA	Special Secretariat for the Environment
SFB	Brazilian Forest Service
SIBRAAR	Brazilian Agro-Traceability System
SINAFLOR	National System for Controlling the Origin of Forest Products
SISBOV	Brazilian Cattle and Buffalo Individual Identification System
SISNAMA	National Environmental System
SME	Small and Medium Enterprises
SNUC	National System of Conservation Units
SPS	Sanitary and Phytosanitary Measures
SSI	Semi-Structured Interview
TBT	Technical Barriers to Trade
TSD	Trade and Sustainable Development
UC	Conservation Units
UF	Federation Unit
UN	United Nations
WTO	World Trade Organization

List of Figures

List of Tables

Chapter 1
Introduction

1.1 Context

As is well known, global deforestation and forest degradation poses a serious and ongoing challenge for the international community.[1] Unsustainable depletion of forests has been acknowledged at international level on several occasions. The United Nations Food and Agricultural Organization (FAO) has confirmed that across regions, particularly in tropical forest areas, deforestation has been occurring over a substantial period, particularly since the 1990s, and has led to a very sizeable if gradually reducing trend rate of net global forest losses, estimated at around 10 million hectares annually.[2]

Forests constitute vitally important ecosystems providing support for biodiversity, as havens for a multiplicity of both fauna and flora, and providing other environmental services such as assisting with enhancing air quality, serving as carbon sinks and as water flow regulators. In addition, they also provide important resources from an economic perspective to human societies, in particular constituting an important source underpinning the livelihood for a relevant proportion of the global population, such as indigenous peoples, local communities and smallholders.

Deforestation and forest degradation have complex, context-dependent causes, but are often linked to the production and trade of agricultural commodities.[3] The link between the international trade of commodities originating from deforested areas and global deforestation underpins a significant portion of worldwide forest loss. Agricultural expansion is the primary driver of deforestation, forest degradation and biodiversity loss.[4] The conversion of forests, particularly in tropical areas rich in biodiversity, into land for farming, grazing, or logging is driven by the demand for

[1] Hedemann-Robinson (2024).

[2] FAO (2024).

[3] Seymour and Harris (2019) and Pacheco et al. (2021).

[4] OECD (2023).

P. Wojcikiewicz Almeida et al., *The Normative and Regulatory Challenges for the Implementation of the European Deforestation-Free Regulation in Third Affected Countries*, https://doi.org/10.1007/978-3-032-08458-3_1

various agricultural and forestry products in consumer markets. This process typically involves clearing forests to establish plantations for crops such as palm oil, soybeans, coffee, and cocoa, or to create pasture for cattle. These commodities then become part of global supply chains, are traded internationally, and are eventually consumed in diverse forms by people and industries around the globe. This worldwide demand generates ongoing economic incentives for land conversion, as producers react to market demands and seek to maximize earnings by increasing their production areas.

Furthermore, the economic incentives within the international trade system can sometimes favour deforestation. Commodities produced on newly cleared land may be cheaper due to lower initial land costs or less stringent environmental regulations in producing countries. This can create a competitive disadvantage for producers who adopt more sustainable, forest-friendly practices, as they may face higher production costs. The lack of robust and universally enforced international regulations on deforestation and sustainable land use further exacerbates this issue, allowing the trade in deforestation-linked commodities to persist and even thrive in certain sectors.

The severe repercussions of international trade in commodities originating from deforested lands underscore the responsibility of major consumer regions in driving this environmental destruction. The European Union (EU), through its consumption of various agricultural imports, has been shown to be a significant contributor to global deforestation. The European Commission determined in 2021 that the Union's consumption of six agricultural commodities from 2008 to 2017 was a significant driver of tropical deforestation, contributing around 19%, with commodities such as coffee, cocoa, soy and palm oil as main drivers.[5] With increasing recognition of its contribution to global deforestation, the EU has formulated a set of measures intended to address its role.

The EU's engagement with forest governance began with the 2003 FLEGT Action Plan, a foundational policy that led to the 2005 FLEGT Regulation and the 2010 EU Timber Regulation, both crucial in combating illegal logging and its associated trade. Building on these initial efforts, the 2019 Commission Communication on Stepping up EU Action to Protect and Restore the World's Forests outlined a more expansive strategy to address deforestation and forest degradation, reinforcing the EU's dedication to mitigating forest-related environmental challenges. This commitment was subsequently solidified within the overarching European Green Deal and the EU Biodiversity Strategy for 2030. Recognizing the inherent limitations of its earlier legislative tools, which primarily concentrated on illegal logging and trade within the existing Union legal framework, and lacked direct mechanisms to tackle deforestation itself, the EU has adopted Regulation (EU) 2023/1115 on deforestation-free products (EUDR), the main focus of this study.

The EU has implemented the EUDR as a key component of its global strategy to combat deforestation and forest degradation. This demand-side measure seeks to reduce greenhouse gas emissions and biodiversity loss by regulating trade in relevant commodities. Building upon the assertion that the main driver of deforestation is the expansion of agricultural land, the EUDR regulates the trade of goods from seven

[5] European Commission (2021).

commodities (cattle, cocoa, coffee, palm oil, rubber, soya, and wood) if they originate from deforested regions. To ensure their supply chains are free from deforestation and forest degradation, market operators and traders must submit due diligence declarations. These declarations include specific information, risk assessments, and any necessary mitigation measures. Operators and traders must comply with these obligations before placing products on the market, and requirements will be influenced by the level of risk assigned to the product's region of origin. The EUDR also includes a three-tier country benchmarking system. This system assesses the risk of producing these commodities and determines whether a country must adhere to both its own regulations and those established by the EUDR.

The EUDR's potential to significantly impact a wide range of stakeholders underscores the need for a multi-level analytical framework to fully understand its implications. This framework must account for the complex interactions between various stakeholders, such as producers, traders, consumers, governments, and civil society organizations, within and across different jurisdictions.

Producing countries are concerned that compliance with the EUDR may negatively impact their production chains and lead to increased trade costs. Although the EUDR does not directly apply to non-EU producing countries, its extraterritorial effects require them to comply with the regulation in order to introduce their products into the EU's market. The authors define the process of third countries adapting their domestic framework to the provisions of the EUDR as 'indirect implementation'. Given its status as a major producer and exporter of commodities, Brazil is concerned about the potential implications of the EUDR and serves as a paradigmatic case study.

Brazil is a major producer of commodities and depends to a large extent on exporting its production.[6] Additionally, the country is home to the world's largest tropical rainforest, the Amazon, and has a history of fighting deforestation. According to the National Inventory of Greenhouse Gas Emissions, land use and forestry, which includes deforestation, are responsible for most of Brazil's greenhouse gas emissions.[7]

On the other hand, corporations will face more stringent regulatory requirements, leading to increased costs and operational complexities. Businesses, across various sectors and within EU member states, have expressed significant concerns regarding the European Commission's guidance on EUDR implementation. While the Commission has released additional guidance by the end of 2024, industry stakeholders argue that this guidance remains unclear and ambiguous in many areas. This lack of clarity creates significant uncertainty for businesses, hindering their ability to effectively plan and comply with the regulation.

Businesses are also worried about the substantial increase in administrative burdens and compliance costs associated with the EUDR. The regulation requires extensive due diligence, supply chain traceability, and risk assessments, which can

[6] Brazil 'Comexstat' (2024) and WTO (2023).

[7] SEEG (2024).

be complex and resource-intensive, particularly for small and medium-sized enterprises (SMEs). This added layer of bureaucracy could significantly impact operational costs and competitiveness. The EUDR may disrupt existing supply chains, particularly for businesses reliant on commodities from regions with high deforestation risk. Ensuring compliance with the regulation's requirements, such as demonstrating deforestation-free sourcing, could lead to supply chain disruptions, delays, and increased costs.

Local producers and communities may also experience disruptions in their production chains, increased costs associated with certification schemes, and potential shifts in market dynamics. However, this book does not delve into the specific impacts on local producers, communities and civil society organizations. It is important to note that the EUDR's original entry into force has been delayed. This delay creates additional challenges to accurately predict its concrete effects on local communities. Furthermore, establishing a clear cause-and-effect relationship between the regulation and its impacts on local communities requires rigorous research methodologies and long-term monitoring.

1.2 Research Questions and Methodology

Given the complexities and potential consequences of the EUDR, this book aims to answer the following question: what are the normative and regulatory challenges policymakers and economic players face when indirectly implementing the EUDR in Brazil?[8]

This question can be disaggregated in the following specific inquiries: (a) what are the key justifications for the EU's unilateral approach, exemplified by trade-related environmental measures like the EUDR, in addressing global deforestation, and how does the 'Brussels Effect' contribute to the potential global impact of such measures?; (b) what are the key challenges and potential areas of incompatibility within Brazil's existing normative and regulatory framework concerning deforestation and forest degradation that may influence the indirect implementation of the EUDR?; (c) how do key stakeholders in the Brazilian coffee sector perceive the challenges and opportunities associated with the indirect implementation of the EUDR?

This research employs a mixed methodological approach to address EUDR's normative and regulatory challenges in Brazil. The study draws on semi-structured interviews (SSIs) as a qualitative method to explore the impacts of the EUDR implementation in Brazil, specifically focusing on the coffee sector. Interviews are considered highly valuable research tools for observing and engaging with specific individuals or groups of interest within a limited timeframe.[9] Specifically, semi-structured

[8] This book aims to capture the state of discussions and developments surrounding the EUDR as of the end of March 2025.

[9] Lodge (2013).

interviews (SSIs) are widely recognized as effective means to address gaps that may arise from the sole use of other research methods, such as the content analysis techniques.[10] SSIs can be described as a qualitative data collection method organized around predefined thematic frameworks but not bound to a fixed order or exact wording of questions.[11] This approach allows for conversations that, while flexible, remain in-depth, methodologically grounded, and aligned with the study's core objectives.

Potential interviewees were identified through stakeholder mapping, targeting public and private actors with key roles in the implementation of the EUDR in Brazil. They were then contacted via email, which included a description of the research project, an invitation to participate, and a consent letter to be signed upon agreement. A total of 13 interviews were conducted between September 2024 and January 2025, following a semi-structured script to ensure alignment with the study's objectives. Public sector participants included representatives from the Ministries of Foreign Affairs; Agriculture, Livestock and Supply; and Environment and Climate Change, as well as individuals from international organizations. From the private sector, interviewees included coffee producers and representatives from coffee exporters and industry associations, encompassing actors working with producers of various scales. The coffee sector was chosen due to its vital role in Brazil's economy, both as a major export commodity and as a driver of rural employment and development. As the world's largest coffee producer and exporter, Brazil holds strong trade ties to the EU.

The interviews conducted with public sector representatives served primarily as a foundation for guiding the research on relevant legislation, compliance mechanisms related to the EUDR, and associated documentation, which is explored on the first and second chapters. In contrast, the interviews with stakeholders from the coffee sector are explicitly explored in this study, offering insights into the perceived on-the-ground impacts of the EUDR's implementation in Brazil and the practical challenges in relation to the EU norm. Thus, the book deeply explores 5 interviews, from the total of 13-, specifically featuring coffee sector's stakeholders who have business presence and\or representational role in Brazil or on the international stage. This analysis is object of the third chapter.

1.3 Structure of the Book

The first chapter focuses on the EU's role as a global standard-setter in regulatory matters and analyses how its policies, particularly those related to climate change and deforestation, can shape environmental regulations and practices worldwide. It begins by examining the shortcomings of existing international and regional legal frameworks in addressing deforestation. This critical analysis highlights the gaps

[10] Lima (2016) and Souliotis (2022).

[11] Pin (2023).

and limitations of current legal instruments in effectively combating deforestation and its associated environmental and social impacts on a global scale. Finally, the chapter delves into the complex issue of unilateral environmental measures and extraterritoriality in international law. This section critically examines the legal basis and implications of EU policies that extend beyond its borders, particularly those aimed at addressing deforestation in other countries.[12] It explores the legal challenges and potential conflicts that may arise from such extraterritorial measures, considering principles of international law such as sovereignty and non-interference in the domestic affairs of third states.

The second chapter examines the main elements of the EUDR and of several previous norms, particularly the FLEGT, the EUTR and the Green Deal. The chapter begins by tracing the road to the EUDR, outlining the political and legislative developments that led to its adoption. This section examines the key drivers behind the regulation, including growing public concern over deforestation, increasing pressure from civil society, and the EU's commitment to combating climate change and biodiversity loss. Next, the chapter conducts a normative analysis of the EUDR, examining its legal basis, scope, and key provisions. This analysis critically evaluates the regulation's objectives, its potential effectiveness in curbing deforestation, and its compatibility with existing international and EU law. Then, it discusses several normative challenges that can lead to potential 'bottlenecks' in trade operations with third countries.

The third chapter explores the implications of the EUDR for international trade, focusing on two key aspects: (i) potential impact on trade flows: this section analyses how the EUDR may affect trade patterns between the EU and other countries, examining potential disruptions to supply chains, shifts in production and consumption patterns, and the potential for trade disputes (using databases such as Brazil's ComexStat and ITC's Trade Map); (ii) contestation at the WTO: this section examines the potential for legal challenges to the EUDR at the World Trade Organization (WTO), considering arguments related to non-discrimination, national treatment, and the use of trade measures for environmental purposes. Finally, the chapter examines the reactions to the EUDR from various stakeholders, including governments, businesses and civil society.

The fourth chapter delves into the specific context of Brazil, examining its unique challenges and opportunities in adapting to the EUDR. It begins by analysing the Brazilian normative and regulatory framework concerning deforestation and forest degradation across various biomes, including forests and non-forest ecosystems. This analysis explores the existing legal and regulatory landscape in Brazil, identifying key legislation, policies, and enforcement mechanisms aimed at combating deforestation. Finally, the chapter focuses on the challenges for implementing the EUDR in the Brazilian context. This section explores specific challenges such as: (i) unclear definitions: potential ambiguities and inconsistencies in the EUDR's definitions of deforestation, forest degradation, and other key terms, which may create difficulties

[12] Hornkohl (2022).

in interpretation and implementation in the Brazilian context; (ii) potential incompatibility with national certification and traceability systems: The potential for conflicts or inconsistencies between the requirements of the EUDR and existing national certification and traceability systems used in Brazil, potentially creating administrative burdens and increasing compliance costs for businesses. The chapter then conducts a deeper look into the coffee sector, a significant commodity sector in Brazil with potential implications for EUDR compliance. This sector-specific analysis examines, via semi-structured interviews, the coffee industry's current practices, supply chains, and existing sustainability certifications and traceability systems. It assesses the potential impacts of the EUDR on the coffee sector, including challenges and opportunities for adaptation and compliance.

Thus far, no book has been published in the English language that comprehensively analyses the indirect implementation of the EUDR in impacted countries through an interdisciplinary normative and regulatory lens. The current state of knowledge largely consists of normative descriptions of the regulatory framework and its history, a limitation this work intends to overcome. By examining the Brazilian case, this research seeks to identify obstacles, map out alternative mechanisms and adaptation measures, and explore potential avenues for discussion to ensure more effective implementation of EU regulations with extraterritorial impact, such as the EUDR.

References

Brazil (2024) Comexstat. https://comexstat.mdic.gov.br/pt/home. Accessed 29 May 2025

European Commission (2021) EU biodiversity strategy for 2030. https://eurlex.europa.eu/resource.html?uri=cellar:a3c806a6-9ab3-11ea-9d2d01aa75ed71a1.0001.02/DOC_1&format=PDF. Accessed 22 Dec 2024

FAO (2024) Strengthening forest-positive agriculture through due diligence. Rome: Food and Agriculture Organization of the United Nations. https://openknowledge.fao.org/items/ec487897-97b5-43ec-bc2e-5ddfc76c8e85/full. Accessed 11 June 2025

Hedemann-Robinson M (2024) Combating deforestation. Edward Elgar Publishing, Cheltenham, UK. https://doi.org/10.4337/9781800888084. Accessed 11 June 2025.

Hornkohl L (2022) The extraterritorial application of statutes and regulations in EU Law. Max Planck Institute Luxembourg for Procedural Law

Lima V (2016) Social mobilisation for housing rights: a qualitative case study using semi-structured interviews. In SAGE Research Methods Cases. https://doi.org/10.4135/978144627305015602461

Lodge M (2013) Semistructured interviews and informal institutions: getting inside executive government. In: Bruter M, Lodge M (eds) Political science research methods in action. Research Methods Series. Palgrave Macmillan, London. https://doi.org/10.1057/9781137318268_9

OECD/FAO (2023) OECD-FAO business handbook on deforestation and due diligence in agricultural supply chains. OECD Publishing, Paris. https://doi.org/10.1787/c0d4bca7-en

Pacheco P, et al (2021) Deforestation fronts, drivers and responses in a changing world: full report. WWF. https://files.worldwildlife.org/wwfcmsprod/files/Publication/file/ocuoxmdil_Deforestation_fronts___drivers_and_responses_in_a_changing_world___full_report__1_.pdf. Accessed 11 June 2025.

Pin C (2023) Semi-structured interviews. LIEPP Methods Brief n°4. Sciences Po. https://sciencespo.hal.science/hal-04087970v1. Accessed 11 June 2025

SEEG (2024) Inventário Nacional de Emissões de Gases de Efeito Estufa do Brasil 2024. SEEG - Sistema de Estimativa de Emissão de Gases. Accessed 22 Nov 2024

Seymour, F Harris, N (2019) Reducing tropical deforestation. Science, American Association for the Advancement of Science. https://doi.org/10.1126/science.aax8546

Souliotis D (2022) Content analysis and semi-structured interviews as assessment tools. In: The European Parliament in the News. Contributions to Political Science. Springer, Cham. https://doi.org/10.1007/978-3-030-93809-3_5

WTO (2023) World Trade Organization, Trade Policy Review Body, Trade Policy Review Report: Brazil (WT/TPR/S/432/Rev.1), 2022. https://docs.wto.org/dol2fe/Pages/SS/directdoc.aspx?filename=q:/WT/TPR/S432R1.pdf&Open=True. Accessed 11 June 2025

Chapter 2
EU as 'Global Standard-Setter' in Climate Change and Effects on Non-EU Countries

In its capacity as a prominent regulatory body and a leading voice in climate diplomacy, the EU has actively pursued a central role in climate change mitigation and financing. This ambition has manifested in a series of EU regulations that establish standards with extraterritorial application, such as the Carbon Border Adjustment Mechanism (CBAM), Corporate Sustainability Reporting Directive (CSRD), Corporate Sustainability Due Diligence Directive (CSDDD) and EUDR. These regulations often establish environmental and sustainability standards that extend their reach and influence beyond the geographical boundaries of the Union's member states. This outward projection of EU norms, a phenomenon recognized as the 'Brussels Effect', underscores the EU's capacity to shape global markets and influence the regulatory landscape in third countries through the sheer power of its market size and regulatory authority.

The Brussels Effect is a theory developed by author Anu Bradford, who in 2012 published an article entitled 'The Brussels Effect' and in 2020 published a book on the same subject.[1] Bradford describes the Brussels Effect as 'unilateral power to regulate global markets without the need to use international institutions or seek other nations' cooperation'.[2] The Brussels Effect, in other words, is a phenomenon in which the EU transports internal trade regulations beyond its borders. Bradford argues that the EU can establish regulations that shape global trade, generating a "'Europeanization' of essential aspects of international trade.[3]

Bradford describes how the EU has long pursued the goals of bloc integration and legal harmonisation through regulation.[4] In time, it also became a deliberate external agenda to establish the EU as 'the global regulatory hegemon'.[5] The externalisation of

[1] Bradford (2020).

[2] Bradford (2020).

[3] Trevizan (2024a).

[4] Bradford (2020).

[5] Bradford (2020).

P. Wojcikiewicz Almeida et al., *The Normative and Regulatory Challenges for the Implementation of the European Deforestation-Free Regulation in Third Affected Countries*, https://doi.org/10.1007/978-3-032-08458-3_2

EU norms and standards beyond its jurisdiction has been possible thanks to its market size, regulatory capacity, and a preference for stringent rules alongside precautionary policymaking.[6] The Brussels Effect suggests that the substantial size of the European market motivate producers and multinational corporations to prioritize adhering to the EU's stringent regulatory standards. To avoid being shut out of this profitable market, these entities often find it more cost-effective to standardize their operations globally to satisfy EU requirements, leading to a worldwide increase in regulatory standards.

The Brussels Effect essentially leads to a unilateral regulatory globalization, in which EU regulations are pursued economically throughout the world market. This effect can occur in two ways: de facto or *de jure*.[7] The de facto Brussels Effect occurs when large companies adjust their production and conduct to the rules set by the EU. The *de jure* Brussels Effect occurs when foreign governments adopt EU regulations; it stems from the de facto Brussels Effect, in that after adjusting, large corporations will lobby their home jurisdictions to adopt European standards. Therefore, the Brussels *de jure* effect often occurs after the Brussels de facto effect, as companies from third countries that have adapted to EU regulations want other companies to do the same so that trade is fair. It is by seeking this justice and adjusting the internal regulatory texts of third countries that the Brussels *de jure* effect will materialize. It should be noted that the Brussels *de jure* effect is a more imposing form of influence, as it involves rearranging an entire existing regulatory system to adapt to new EU standards.

Critics, however, have questioned the EU's extensive regulatory reach. Concerns exist regarding the blurred distinction between the 'Brussels Effect'—a driver of regulatory convergence—and potential trade protectionism.[8] This effect also raises competition concerns,[9] as increased compliance costs could exclude SMEs from the EU market and marginalize them globally, leaving them with limited options. Considering the rising compliance costs, SMEs may have to give up access to the EU market, which would make them marginalised in the global supply chain. In this regard, the extensive impact posed by the Brussels Effect reduces the options of SMEs that might have to make a 'take it or leave it' choice. Moreover, the Brussels Effect may disadvantage developing countries and emerging economies since they may have limited resources to adapt to EU standards.[10]

---

[6] Bradford (2020).

[7] Bradford (2020).

[8] Trevizan (2024b).

[9] Niebel (2021).

[10] Hadjiyianni (2017, p. 263).

2.1 Drivers of Increased EU Climate Action

At least two factors underpin the EU's strategic decision to adopt unilateral trade-related environmental measures within its climate policy framework. Firstly, a significant impetus stems from the lack of a comprehensive and legally binding international framework for global forest protection. Secondly, the perceived limitations or insufficient impact of other EU initiatives in effectively addressing deforestation and its associated environmental consequences have further motivated this policy direction.

Despite the multiple processes and international institutions involved, the international forest regime still does not have a binding multilateral convention. The absence of such agreement has led to separated regulations on forest issues and sustainable forest management in different environmental agreements not designed to address forests. Today, binding and non-binding instruments applicable for forest protection coexist with a set of actors in global forest governance involved in such regulatory activity.[11] These instruments, when considered together, provide for a complex, multi-layered set of values, objectives, principles, obligations, guidelines, recommendations, rules of procedure, decisions, resolutions from international and non-governmental organizations, treaty organs, standard-setting and certification businesses, establishing a 'multi-instrument approach' to international forest regulation.[12]

International regulation concerning particularly forest protection only began to be established in the middle of the last century. The early stages of forest law and policy are marked by the perception of forests as providers of timber. Timber was regarded as a re-growing resource that can be exploited without much difficulty. Thus, forests are perceived as a natural resource under the sovereignty of states, and as such forests can be dealt with at states' discretion. With the establishment of the IUFRO—the International Union of Forest Research Organizations—in 1892 and its mission to investigate and collect knowledge about the ecological, economic and social aspects of forests, forests came under increased international monitoring and assessment. Nevertheless, forests remained a rather untouched issue during the early stages of recognition of international environmental concerns. In 1945 the newly developed specialized agency of the United Nations for Food and Agriculture (FAO) obtained a general forest mandate and thus, the foundation was laid to incorporated forest issues in the United Nations agenda.

International environmental concerns gained considerable momentum with the 1972 Stockholm UN Conference on the Human Environment and the resulting Stockholm Declaration. Despite the lack of a formal acknowledgment of the forest issue, the Stockholm Declaration merits consideration with regard to the fundamental recognition of environmental liability given the elaborations on the relation between the

[11] Restrepo (2023, p. 9).

[12] Eikermann (2015, p. 147).

sovereign right of States to exploit their own resources pursuant to their own environmental policies, and the responsibility thereby not to cause harm for States or areas beyond their national jurisdiction in its Principle 21.

International regulation in the 1970s has also addressed forests within specific frameworks, notably through the 1973 Convention on International Trade in Endangered Species of Wild Fauna and Flora ('CITES') concerning the trade of forest components, the 1971 Ramsar Convention on Wetlands of International Importance Especially as Waterfowl Habitat ('Ramsar Convention') regarding nature conservation and wildlife protection, and the 1972 Convention concerning the Protection of the World Cultural and Natural Heritage ('World Heritage Convention').

Another key step involved the creation of the International Tropical Timber Organization (ITTO) in 1985, following the first International Tropical Timber Agreement (ITTA) in 1983. The ITTA is an international trade agreement designed primarily to '[provide] an effective framework for consultation, international cooperation and policy development among all members with regard to all relevant aspects of the world timber economy (…)'. The ITTA developed in three major negotiation processes from the ITTA 1983, to the ITTA 1994 and the most recent ITTA 2006. Despite being established as an agreement specifically addressing forests, the ITTA merits attention due to the fact that the ITTA does not apply to forests in general, but only to trade in tropical timber. The ITTA is thus doubly limited: firstly, with regard to its regional scope and secondly, in terms of the regulated substance. In this sense, the ITTA is of limited significance for forests in general in three respects: firstly, it is limited in regional scope given is applicable to tropical forests only. Secondly, it is limited in its coverage of forest components because it applies to timber only. Thirdly, it is limited in its protective scope, as its primary objective is the expansion of trade. Ultimately, the ITTA should not be faulted for failing to prevent tropical deforestation or forest degradation. Environmental concerns were never central to its legally binding obligations; instead, it was designed as a commodity agreement to facilitate international trade in tropical timber, not for intrinsic forest protection.

The 1990s saw increasing attention to forests within the context of broader environmental concerns like desertification, biodiversity loss, and climate change. The 1992 United Nations Conference on Environment and Development (UNCED), also known as 'ECO-92' or 'Rio 92', marked a significant turning point for environmental protection. It produced a combination of non-binding and binding instruments. The non-binding outcomes of Rio 92 included 'Agenda 21', the 'Rio Declaration on Environment and Development',[13] and the 'Declaration of Principles on Forests'.[14] In terms of legally binding agreements related to forests, Rio 92 led to the creation of the 'Convention on Biological Diversity' (CBD), the 'United Nations Convention to Combat Desertification' (UNCCD), and the 'United Nations Framework Convention on Climate Change' (UNFCCC).

In the 2000s, the Economic and Social Council of the UN (ECOSOC) established the United Nations Forum on Forests (UNFF) as a subsidiary body with the primary

[13] UN (1992a).

[14] UN (1992b).

objective to promote the management, conservation and sustainable development of all types of forests and to strengthen long-term political commitment to this end. In addition, new legal instruments have been adopted to protect forests, in particular in the form of UN General Assembly (UNGA) resolutions, such as the Non-legally Binding Instrument on All Types of Forests[15] and the UN Strategic Plan for Forests 2017–2030.[16]

In 2015, UNGA Resolution 70/1 adopted the 'UN Agenda 2030 for Sustainable Development',[17] which established targets to be achieved in the environmental, economic, social and institutional domains by 2030. In particular, Sustainable Development Goal 15 aims to "protect, restore and promote sustainable use of terrestrial ecosystems, sustainably manage forests, combat desertification, and halt and reverse land degradation and halt biodiversity loss".

In 2021, during UNFCCC 's 26th Conference of Parties (COP 26), 140 State-Parties signed the 'Glasgow Leaders' Declaration on Forests and Land Use', also known as the 'Forest Deal',[18] which provides a non-binding commitment to halting deforestation and forest degradation by 2030. It also emphasizes the importance of sustainable forest management, conservation, restoration, and financing for achieving this goal. In 2023, Brazil proposed in the COP 28 the Tropical Forest Finance Facility (TFFF) as a global forest fund.[19] This proposal, which is expected to be officially launched at COP 30 in Brazil,[20] provides for funding to 80 countries with tropical forests to help maintain their trees, with annual payments based on the hectares conserved or restored.

The international environmental protection framework has advanced in recent decades, yet a more precise approach to forest protection is still needed.[21] Despite providing considerable substance, the multi-instrument approach suffers from notable shortcomings. These include, firstly, the scattering of essential regulatory content across instruments of varying legal weight, namely non-legally binding and legally binding international treaties. Secondly, the content is disproportionately distributed, as the core principles and goals for comprehensive forest regulation are found in non-legally binding instruments, while legally binding agreements lack specific forest-related provisions, resulting in a regulatory gap.

Furthermore, beyond the absence of a specific global framework for forest protection, the EU's pronounced unilateral approach to combating deforestation can also be attributed to the perceived limitation of the voluntary Partnership Agreements (VPAs) under the FLEGT Regulation in effectively halting European imports of illegal timber from tropical countries.

---

15 UNGA (2008).

16 UNGA (2017).

17 UNGA (2015).

18 UN (2012).

19 Reuters (2013).

20 Brazil (2024).

21 Eikermann (2015).

FLEGT VPAs have shown to be challenging for partner country governments, both politically and administratively, in terms of their demands for multi-stakeholder participation and far-reaching reforms of forest governance.[22] Some of the key implementation challenges concern the practical difficulties of designing effective timber-tracking and legality systems under developing country conditions, but others stem from the prevalence in many countries of entrenched patron-client relations., as well as from pervasive weaknesses in domestic administrative coordination and governance capacity. In every partner country, ensuring timber legality has turned out to be connected to sensitive political issues concerning the exploitation of natural resources, property rights, land use, and state-society relations, which the VPA implementation process has progressively exposed to public scrutiny.

As a result of these challenges, the fulfillment of VPA commitments and the issuance of FLEGT export licenses have taken much longer than expected in all partner countries. In Indonesia, the first to complete the VPA process, export of FLEGT-licensed timber began in 2016. In Ghana, the issuance of FLEGT licenses is expected to start in 2025, almost twenty years after the negotiations began. Liberia has not met the requirements for the FLEGT license, though it has been 11 years since it signed the VPA. In Cameroon, however, VPA implementation has largely stalled amid reports of extensive illegal logging, despite significant progress in terms of transparency and civil society participation in forest governance.

The relevant challenges across the VPA countries include political culture, weak and inconsistent legal framework, legitimacy factors, inadequate law enforcement, inadequate human and financial resources, and a lack of a fully functional data management system.[23] First, the constraints on realized capacity embedded in the political culture of Cameroon, Congo, Ghana, and Liberia have stalled VPA progress to date. This political culture in the forestry sector relates to the abuse of authority by powerful elites and corrupt practices by government officials. Second, in a fragmented governance regime, weak and inconsistent legal framework (e.g., conflicts between formal and informal customary laws related to tree tenure) and poor coordination among different sectors and agencies of government are still a challenge. Third, forest information is poorly disseminated between levels of government because of low political will to collect and manage information, poor documentation, and a lack of strict adherence to the reporting guidelines set out in the VPAs. Fourth, despite the progress made in establishing legal, policy, and institutional frameworks in all five VPA countries, effective compliance monitoring is still limited because of insufficient capacity for law enforcement and weak coordination among national law enforcement agencies.

These limitations in multilateral and voluntary efforts provide a rationale for the EU's more assertive, unilateral regulatory stance, pushing it to adopt measures like the EUDR to directly address deforestation linked to the consumption of commodities within its market, thereby seeking to achieve environmental goals that existing international and cooperative mechanisms have fallen short of delivering. This proactive

---

[22] Overdevest and Zeitlin (2018, p. 68).

[23] Adams et al. (2020).

approach reflects a growing recognition within the EU that relying solely on non-binding agreements and voluntary partnerships is insufficient to tackle the urgent global challenge of deforestation and its environmental consequences, necessitating more direct and impactful regulatory interventions.[24]

2.2 Conceptual Framework

This book employs the conceptual frameworks of unilateral trade-related environmental measures and extraterritoriality as analytical lenses through which to examine the EUDR and its ramifications in third countries. Consequently, this subsection will delve into the fundamental principles and underlying logic of these two crucial concepts.

2.2.1 Unilateral Trade-Related Environmental Measures

Although a universally agreed definition is absent, common dictionary definitions offer initial insight into the usage of unilateralism, according to which it refers to the 'tendency of nations to conduct their foreign affairs individualistically, characterized by minimal consultation and involvement with other nations, even their allies'.[25] To further clarify the concept of unilateral legal action, it is useful to contrast it with the principles of 'multilateralism' and international cooperation. This comparative approach allows for a preliminary definition: unilateral legal action can be understood as the manifestation of the will of a single state or a limited group of states, enacted without the explicit consent of the states that are thereby affected.[26]

The EU employs a range of legal mechanisms and regulatory techniques to project its influence externally, including the adoption of unilateral measures that extend its regulatory reach to processes occurring beyond its territorial borders. While these extraterritorial applications of EU law are increasingly observed across various policy domains, such as financial services regulation and data protection law, this book specifically focuses on their growing significance and prevalence in the critical areas of environmental protection and climate change. Examples of unilateral trade-related environmental measures include the sustainability criteria for biofuels, the inclusion of aviation emissions in the European Union Emissions Trading System (EU ETS), regulation of ship recycling, exports of waste of electrical and electronic equipment, imports of timber (governed by the EU Timber Regulation before being superseded by the EUDR), and imports of fish and fishery products, the CBAM, the CSDDD, the CSRD and the EUDR.

---

[24] Muradian et al. (2025).

[25] Bodansky (2000, p. 339).

[26] Vranes (2009, pp. 173–174).

The legal framework of these measures, aimed at influencing conduct partly occurring outside the EU, operates through at least two mechanisms.[27] Firstly, some measures condition access to the EU market on the basis of production processes in third countries, as seen in timber import regulations. This regulation of extraterritorial conduct via process standards does not always mean imposing EU standards; it can also involve the EU indirectly exerting regulatory influence over processes abroad. For instance, to access the EU market, the EUDR requires that imported regulated commodities are of non-deforested origin, and it controls this access by referencing the legality standards of the producing country.

2.2.2 Extraterritoriality

The term ‘unilateralism’ is often associated with the concept of extraterritorial jurisdiction.[28] Extraterritoriality’ is a widely discussed concept within international legal scholarship, characterized by its multiple meanings[29] and broad application across fields such as legal pluralism, international trade law, international investment law, international human rights law, and state responsibility.

The International Law Commission (ILC), in a 2006 report on extraterritorial jurisdiction, refers to extraterritoriality as "‘an attempt to regulate by means of national legislation, adjudication or enforcement the conduct of persons, property or acts beyond its borders’.[30] A similar definition appears in the Max Planck Encyclopedia of Public International Law, which specifies that ‘the terms ‘extraterritoriality’ and ‘extraterritorial jurisdiction’ refer to the competence of a State to make, apply and enforce rules of conduct in respect of persons, property or events beyond its territory’.[31]

In line with the usual division of branches of government, public power that is projected extraterritorially can consist of legislative, executive or judicial power. From the perspective of this book, particular interest is given to the legislative power (usually referred to as legislative or prescriptive jurisdiction) that is exercised by the EU institutions by virtue of the normative competences conferred on them by Member States and that is reflected in the unilateral adoption of autonomous legal instruments, such as regulations, directives and decisions.

The term extraterritoriality is sometimes seen to have pejorative connotations,[32] since State sovereignty has strong territorial roots.[33] Indeed, as the Permanent Court of International Justice (PCIJ) already noted in its 1927 *Lotus* case, states are political

[27] Hadjiyianni (2017, p. 176).

[28] Vranes (2009, p. 173).

[29] Meessen (1996) and Parrish and Ryngaert (2023).

[30] International Law Commission (2006, p. 229).

[31] Kamminga (2020).

[32] Dobson (2021, p. 38) and Ryngaert (2015, p. 8).

[33] Kohen (2016) and Bonet Pérez (2022).

entities with a territorial basis and their sovereignty is projected, in principle, over the persons, property and acts located within their territory.[34] However, this does not exclude that a State's powers (or, more recently, the powers of international integration organizations such as the EU) may in certain cases be projected beyond its territory if this is compatible with international law, which is the legal system entrusted with the allocation of spheres of jurisdiction among the various sovereign States.[35] The ILC underlines that customary international law recognizes certain bases or principles that allow States to regulate extraterritorially, including, for example, the active nationality principle, the passive nationality principle, the protective principle and the effects doctrine.[36] Thus, in contemporary international law, one trend is to broaden the bases for the adoption of legislation with an extraterritorial reach as a consequence of many factors,[37] such as the globalization of the economy, the increase in transnational crime and cybercrime and global environmental challenges.

Therefore, the characterization of a measure as extraterritorial is a legally neutral one, which does not, per se, imply that the measure is against international law.[38] While there may be extraterritorial measures that are deemed internationally unlawful, other measures that can be deemed fully compatible with international law if they have a basis or principle that effectively supports them. According to the ILC, the common element underlying the various principles for the extraterritorial exercise of jurisdiction by a State under international law is the valid interest of the State in asserting its jurisdiction in such a case on the basis of a sufficient connection to the persons, property or acts concerned.[39]

The EU has adopted a wide range of measures that seek to reduce the environmental pressures and impacts that are embodied in EU trade. These measures make access to the EU market, and to other advantages conferred by the EU or its Member States, conditional upon compliance with environmental standards included in EU law. This includes environmental standards that govern methods or harvesting or producing goods abroad. There is ongoing discussion on whether these trade-related environmental measures constitute an example of extraterritoriality.[40]

Scott argues that these measures constitute examples of 'territorial extension' in EU law in that they use the existence of a territorial connection with the EU (e.g. market access) to gain regulatory leverage over conduct that takes place abroad.[41]

Article 52 of the Treaty on the European Union (TEU) and Article 355 of the Treaty on the Functioning of the European Union (TFEU) specify the territorial scope of application of EU treaties: the territory of EU Member States with specific rules concerning overseas territories. Those provisions—which must be read in light

---

[34] PCIJ (1927, p. 18).

[35] PCIJ (1927, p. 9).

[36] International Law Commission (2006, p. 231).

[37] International Law Commission (2006, p. 229).

[38] Dobson (2021, p. 7).

[39] International Law Commission (2006, p. 231).

[40] Vranes (2009).

[41] J. Scott and Rajamani (2012) and Cremona and Scott (2019).

of Article 29 of the Vienna Convention on the Law of Treaties (VCLT) specifying that a treaty is generally binding upon each party in respect of its entire territory—were primarily relevant to determine the *ratione loci* of the rights and obligations of EU Member States.[42] However, the Court of Justice of the European Union (CJEU) has relied on Articles 52 TEU and 355 TFEU to consider that 'in the absence of detail as to the territorial scope of an act of secondary legislation, that scope must be determined on the basis of those provisions, since the secondary legislation applies in principle to the same area as the Treaties themselves'.[43] As Advocate General Jääskinen noted, 'an EU legislative measure cannot be invalid simply because it has effects on conduct in territory located outside of the EU'.[44] In that regard, 'the decisive element from an international law perspective is that the particular facts display a sufficient link with the State or international organisation concerned'.

References

Bodansky D (2000) What's so bad about unilateral action to protect the environment? Eur J Int L 11(2):339–347. https://doi.org/10.1093/ejil/11.2.339

Bonet Pérez J (2022) Jurisdição e obrigações jurídicas internacionais do Estado em matéria de direitos econômicos, sociais e culturais, Revista Eletrônica da Faculdade de Direito da Universidade Federal de Pelotas 8 (1)

Bradford A (2020) The Brussels effect: how the European Union rules the world, 1st edn. Oxford University Press. https://doi.org/10.1093/oso/9780190088583.001.0001

Brazil (2024) COP30: Brazil works to consolidate diplomatic leadership in climate agenda. https://www.gov.br/secom/en/latest-news/2024/12/cop30-brazil-works-toconsolidate-diplomatic-leadership-in-climate-agenda. Accessed 22 December 2024

Convention on Biological Diversity [CDB] (2011) Convention on biological diversity. https://www.cbd.int/convention/text. Accessed 22 February 2024

Court of Justice of the EU, Case C-17/16, Oussama El Dakkak, ECLI:EU:C:2017:341, § 23

Court of Justice of the EU, Opinion of Advocate General Jääskinen, Case C-507/13, United Kingdom v Parliament and Council, ECLI:EU:C:2014:2394, § 36

Cremona M, Scott J (2019) The global reach of EU Law. In: EU law beyond EU borders: Teh extraterritorial reach of EU Law. Oxford University Press, UK. https://doi.org/10.1093/oso/9780198842170.001.0001

Cremona M (2019) Extending the reach of EU Law: the EU as an international legal actor. In EU law beyond EU borders. Oxford University Press, pp 64–111. https://doi.org/10.1093/oso/9780198842170.003.0003

Dobson N (2021) Extraterritoriality and climate change jurisdiction: exploring EU climate protection under international law. Hart, Oxford

Eikermann A (2015) Forests in international law: is there really a need for an international forest convention? Springer International Publishing, Cham. https://doi.org/10.1007/978-3-319-14950-9

Fox H (1996) Extraterritorial jurisdiction in theory and practice, in: Meessen KM (ed). Kluwer Law International

[42] Cremona (2019).

[43] CJEU (2017).

[44] CJEU (2014).

Hadjiyianni I (2017) The extraterritorial reach of EU Environmental Law and access to justice by third country actors. Eur Pape J L Integr 2:519–542. https://doi.org/10.15166/2499-8249/167

International Law Commission (2006) Extraterritorial jurisdiction. International Law Commission

Kamminga MT (2020) Extraterritoriality. In: Planck M (ed) Encyclopedia of public international law. Oxford University Press

Kohen M (2016) Territoriality and International Law. Edward Elgar. https://www.e-elgar.com/shop/usd/territoriality-and-international-law-9781783472383.html. Accessed 27 May 2025

Marshall Alhassan Adams et al (2020) A comparative analysis of the institutional capacity of FLEGT VPA in Cameroon, the Central African Republic, Ghana, Liberia, and the Republic of the Congo 112 Forest Policy and Economics 148 https://linkinghub.elsevier.com/retrieve/pii/S1389934118306051. Accessed 25 April 2025

Muradian R, Cahyafitri R, Ferrando T, Grottera C, Jardim-Wanderley L, Krause T, et al (2025) Will the EU deforestation-free products regulation (EUDR) reduce tropical forest loss? Insights from three producer countries. Ecol Econ:227.https://doi.org/10.1016/j.ecolecon.2024.108389

Niebel C (2021) The impact of the general data protection regulation on innovation and the global political economy. Comput Law Secur Rev 40:105523. https://doi.org/10.1016/j.clsr.2020.105523

Overdevest C, Zeitlin J (2018) Experimentalism in transnational forest governance: Implementing European Union Forest Law Enforcement, Governance and Trade (FLEGT) Voluntary Partnership Agreements in Indonesia and Ghana. Regul Govern 12(1):64–87. https://doi.org/10.1111/rego.12180

Parrish A, Ryngaert C (2023) Research handbook on extraterritoriality in international law, in: Parrish A, Ryngaert C (ed). Edward Elgar Publishing

Permanent Court of International Justice - PCIJ (1927) The Case of the S.S. "Lotus," – Judgment, September 7, 1927 (Lotus Judgment). https://archive.org/details/5975731-National-Security-Archive-Permanent-Court-of. Accessed 22 May 2025.

Restrepo YVP (2023) Regime interaction in international forest law: the role of secondary law of forest-related multilateral environmental agreements. Brill | Nijhoff. https://doi.org/10.1163/9789004678040

Reuters (2013) Brazil proposes global forest conservation fund at COP28. https://www.reuters.com/business/environment/brazil-proposes-global-forest-conservationfund-cop28-2023-12-01/. Accessed 22 February 2024

Ryngaert C (2015) Jurisdiction in international law, 2nd edn. Oxford University Press, Oxford

Scott J, Rajamani L (2012) EU climate change unilateralism. Eur J Int L 23(2):469–494. https://doi.org/10.1093/ejil/chs020

Trevizan AF (2024a) Exploring the Brussels effect: the European Union's impact on brazilian forestry policies. Revista de Direito 16(01):01–25. https://doi.org/10.32361/2024160116014

Trevizan AF (2024b) Exploring the Brussels effect: the European Union's impact on Brazilian forestry policies. Revista de Direito, Universidade Federal de Viçosa 16(1)

United Nations (1983) International Tropical Timber Agreement. chromeextension://efaidnbmnnnibpcajpcglclefindmkaj/https://treaties.un.org/doc/Publication/UNTS/Volume%201393/volume-1393-A-23317-English.pdf. Accessed 22 February 2024

United Nations (1992) Declaration of principles on forests. https://www.un.org/documents/ga/conf151/aconf15126-3annex3.htm. Accessed 22 February 2024

United Nations (1992) Report of the United Nations Conference on Environment and Development, 'Rio Declaration on Environment'

United Nations (1996) United Nations Convention to Combat Desertification in Those Countries Experiencing Serious Drought and/or Desertification, Particularly in Africa (UNCCD). https://treaties.un.org/Pages/ViewDetails.aspx?src=IND&mtdsg_no=XXVII10&chapter=27&clang=_en. Accessed 22 February 2024

United Nations (2008) General Assembly, Non-legally binding instrument on all types of forests, A/RES/62/98.

United Nations (2012) 28th UN Climate Change Conference of Parties. Glasgow Leaders' Declaration in Forest and Land Use. https://ukcop26.org/glasgow-leadersdeclaration-on-forests-and-land-use/. Accessed 6 March 2024

United Nations (2015) General assembly, transforming our world: the 2030 Agenda for Sustainable Development, A/RES/70/1

United Nations (2017) General Assembly, United Nations strategic plan for forests 2017–2030, A/RES/71/285

Vranes E (2009) 'Unilateralism' in the Trade and Environment Context. In: Trade and the environment, 1st ed,. Oxford University Press, Oxford, pp 172–184. https://doi.org/10.1093/acprof:oso/9780199562787.003.0006

World Trade Organization (2022) Trade Policy Review: Brazil (No. WT/TPR/S/432). https://www.wto.org/english/tratop_e/tpr_e/s432_sum_e.pdf. Accessed 27 May 2025

Chapter 3
Assessing the EUDR'S Challenges and Opportunities

3.1 The Road to the EUDR

Since the late 2000s, the EU has developed its environmental policy through a series of comprehensive legislative packages.[1] First initiatives aimed to construct a specific framework for forest regulation in the EU territory. Later, and under a broader scope brought by the Green Deal, the EU fostered policies to also tackle third countries by regulating its own market vis-à-vis the EU own economic power.

3.1.1 The FLEGT and the EUTR

Even before the EUDR, a notorious EU's contemporary milestone on forest protection is the 'EU's Forest Law Enforcement Governance and Trade (FLEGT) Action Plan'. The FLEGT Action Plan sets out a range of measures to tackle illegal logging in the world's forests within the EU, such as supporting timber-producing countries; promoting trade in legal timber; promoting environmentally and socially beneficial public procurement policies; supporting private-sector initiatives; financing and investment safeguards; using existing or new legislation; and addressing the problem of conflict timber. More specifically, the FLEGT Action Plan led to two key pieces of

[1] Gheuens (2023, p. 50).

Natália da Silva Barcelos, former researcher of the FGV Rio Law's Centre for Global Law and PhD student and Master in Sociology at the Institute of Social and Political Studies (IESP-UERJ), is a contributing author to this chapter.

P. Wojcikiewicz Almeida et al., *The Normative and Regulatory Challenges for the Implementation of the European Deforestation-Free Regulation in Third Affected Countries*, https://doi.org/10.1007/978-3-032-08458-3_3

Country	Date of entry into force of agreement	Date of ratification of agreement	Date of signature of agreement	Start of FLEGT licensing
Honduras	2022	2021	2021	
Vietnam	2019	2019	2018	
Indonesia	2014	2014	2013	2016
Liberia	2013	2013	2011	
Congo	2013	2013	2010	
Cameroon	2011	2011	2010	
Central African Republic	2012	2012	2011	
Ghana	2009	2024	2009	June 2025
Democratic Republic of the Congo	[Under negotiations]			
Côte d'Ivoire			2024	
Gabon	[Under negotiations]			
Guyana	[Under negotiations]		2022	

Fig. 3.1 FLEGT voluntary partnership agreements on forest law enforcement, governance and trade (up to January 2025)

legislation: the FLEGT Licensing Scheme (2005) [2] and the EU Timber Regulation or EUTR (2010).[3]

The FLEGT Licensing Scheme apply only to imports from partner countries[4] and aim to confirm that a shipment of timber or timber products complies with EU due diligence requirements. Nevertheless, only Indonesia had fully implemented the schemes.[5] In Indonesia, FLEGT licensing authorities are independent organisations registered with the Ministry of Environment and Forestry. To obtain a FLEGT license, the exporter applies in writing to the licensing authority with which it holds a contract and, if approved, the scheme is issued. Thus, the authority of the country of origin gives a guarantee to the exporter and importer as to the legality of the operation on the basis of terms agreed with the EU. Figure 3.1 shows the FLEGT Voluntary Partnership Agreements on Forest Law Enforcement, Governance and Trade.

While the FLEGT Licensing Scheme has its own dynamic, the EUTR is closer to how the EUDR seeks to work.[6] To summarise, the 2010 norm aims to lay down obligations to operators who place timber and timber products on the EU's internal

[2] EUR-Lex'Council Regulation (EC) No 2173/2005 of 20 December 2005 on the establishment of a FLEGT licensing scheme for imports of timber into the European Community' (2005) < https://eur-lex.europa.eu/eli/reg/2005/2173/oj/eng > accessed 22 December 2024.

[3] EUR-Lex,'Regulation (EU) No 995/2010 of the European Parliament and of the Council of 20 October 2010 laying down the obligations of operators who place timber and timber products on the market' (2010) < https://eur-lex.europa.eu/eli/reg/2010/995/oj/eng > accessed 22 December 2024.

[4] See list in Annex I.

[5] FLEGT License,'Indonesian FLEGT licensing procedures' (2025) < https://www.flegtlicence.org/th/indonesian-flegt-licensing-procedures.html accessed 05 January 2025 > .

[6] In fact, Article 37 of the EUDR states that the EUTR will be repealed by its full entry into force since its scope is included in that of the EUDR. See further comparison in Annex II.

market for the first time, as well to traders.[7] These obligations are related to the prohibition of placing on the EU market of illegally harvested timber or timber products and the need to provide due diligence information.[8]

With more than ten years in force, the EUTR has rarely been used to penalise a company. Yet, an emblematic case was Oceanco's breach of the EUTR in 2022, which came to an end by December 2024.[9] Oceanco, one of the world 's biggest boat builder, was fined more than €150,000 by the Netherlands Public Prosecution Service for breaking the EUTR's requirements. The decision came few days after similar case with Sunseeker for violating the post-Brexit United Kingdom Timber Regulation (UKTR).[10]

In the case, Oceanco was found guilty of using illegal teak in furniture and interior finishings aboard the boat Koru, owned by Amazon's CEO Jeff Bezos. Despite the claims of unintentional breach of the EUTR, the company was found guilty due to being the first to place the timber on the EU market and not being able to conclusively verify whether the wood had been legally or illegally harvested.

Another notorious episode was EC's sanctions alert on high risk of circumvention of illegal plywood imports[11] originated from Russia and Belarius.[12] On 14 March 2025, the EC issued the alert to enhance due diligence on the origin of imported plywood, particularly by a stronger application of the EUTR. The alert came just after the release of the report 'Blood-stained Birch'[13] by the non-governmental organization (NGO) Earthsight.

While both FLEGT and the EUTR remained the most relevant EU regulations on forest protection for more than 10 years, EU guidelines regarding environment themes were update in 2019 by the European Green Deal.[14] This set of policies and strategies brought legal binding climate targets covering all key sectors of the economy and including emissions reduction targets across a broad range of sectors, a target to boost natural carbon sinks, an updated emissions trading system to cap emissions, put a price on pollution and generate investments in the green transition, and social support for citizens and small businesses.

---

[7] See Article 1 of the EUTR.

[8] See Articles 3 and 4 of the EUTR.

[9] Ross (2024).

[10] Sabillo (2024).

[11] European Commission (2025a, b).

[12] EU sanctions prohibit the purchase, import or transfer, directly or indirectly, of plywood and other wood products originating in Russia or Belarus, or exported from there.

[13] Earthsight (2025).

[14] European Commission (2019).

3.1.2 The Green Deal

The Green Deal is considered a new growth strategy,[15] yet some authors understand that the Green Deal is best remarked as a continuation and at worst backsliding compared to previous legislation regarding EU GHG emission objectives.[16]

The Green Deal is divided in several main policy areas[17]: 'Climate change: what the EU is doing'; 'Fit for 55'; 'Circular economy'; 'Nature restoration'. These goals are set out in the 'European Climate Law', particularly concerning a legally binding target of net zero greenhouse gas emissions by 2050[18] and are operationalized by more specific norms. These norms can be divided into three groups of policies[19]: those that concern direct financial impact, those related to transparency and reporting, and those relating to value chains, such as the EUDR. These norms bring updates and directives to the implementation of the Green Deal.

As one of the main building blocks of the Green Deal, the Circular Economy Action Plan[20] introduces legislative and non-legislative measures which target how products are designed, promote circular economy processes, encourage sustainable consumption, and ensure that waste is prevented and the resources used are 'kept' in the EU economy for as long as possible. This includes, inter alia, making sustainable products the norm in the EU and focusing on the sectors that use most resources and where the potential for circularity is high. Based on these objectives, the EU fostered market-based measures to regulate circulation of products with potential environmental impacts by mainly establishing due diligence requirements.

The Green Deal also promoted other scope-specific regulations. For instance, in 2021, the EU Biodiversity Strategy for 2030[21] brought a long-term plan to protect nature and reverse the degradation of ecosystems. The strategy aims to put Europe's biodiversity on a path to recovery by 2030 regarding themes such as the impacts of climate change, forest fires, food insecurity, and disease outbreaks, which includes the protection of wildlife and fighting illegal wildlife trade. Another example is the Nature Restoration Law,[22] a proposal that aims to set a legal standard for EU Member States to restore 20% of degraded land and sea ecosystems by 2030. The regulation is the most recent from the European Green Deal that is intended to mitigate the impacts of climate change and, regarding to the forestry sector, the law specifically identifies 'close-to-nature' and 'continuous cover' perspectives. It also provides for an increase in regulations for the agricultural sector. Examples of the norms set out in the Green Deal can be found in the Fig. 3.2.

---

[15] Biscosi (2025).

[16] Gheuens (2023).

[17] European Council (2024a, b).

[18] Regulation (EU) 2021/1119 (2021), Art. 4.

[19] Damsté et al. (2024), EUR-Lex (2021b).

[20] European Commission (2024a, b, c, d, e).

[21] European Commission (2021).

[22] European Commission (2024a, b, c, d, e).

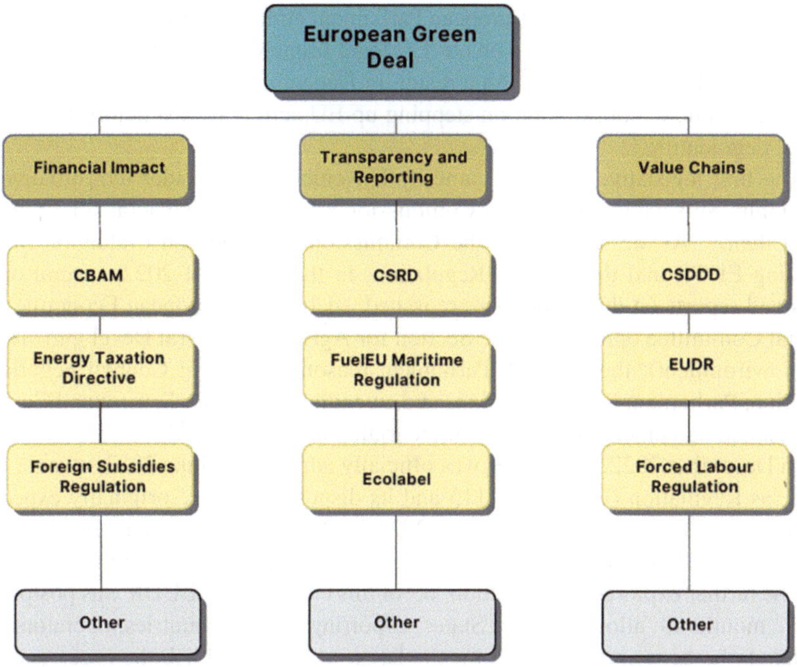

Fig. 3.2 Examples of norms under the Green Deal

However, the Green Deal is not free from criticisms, as it has been targeted by farmers, companies, public opinion and governments, who are questioning it and calling for a regulatory pause.[23] Also, some studies found that the Green Deal had only mixed progress so far.[24]

3.1.3 The EUDR

The EUDR was created under the EU regulatory framework on the environment (spearheaded by the Green Deal) and, more precisely, related to forest-risk commodities (FRC).[25] Its scope was first discussed in June 2020, with the introduction of a framework for feedback on the initiative to tackle global deforestation.[26] Later in

[23] Malingre (2024).

[24] European Commission (2024a, b, c, d, e).

[25] EUR-Lex (2021a).

[26] European Parliament (2019).

October of the same year, the European Parliament emitted a resolution with recommendations to the Commission on an 'EU legal framework to halt and reverse EU-driven global deforestation'.[27] As a result, in December, the European Commision launched a public consultation on stepping up EU action against deforestation and forest degradation.[28]

The first legislative proposal came by November 2021, under the initiative of Virginijus Sinkevičius, European Commission's Directorate-General for Environment then.[29] At the same time, the Commission published an evaluation of the existing EUTR and the FLEGT Regulation. In the course of 2022, several opinions and reports on the proposal were issued, such as the European Economic and Social Committee opinion (by the Section for Agriculture, Rural Development and the Environment); the Swedish Parliament reasoned opinion; Council negotiated position; Parliament Report, positions and amendments; and Parliament and Council provisional agreement and the text of the trialogue agreement.[30]

In December 2022, the EUDR was officially adopted. In June 2023, it came into force as Regulation (EU) 2023/1115 and its dispositions were originally expected to come into force only in December 2024 for larger business and June 2025 for small and medium enterprises (SME). Yet, after much international criticism (which will be further explored in subsection 'd.' of this chapter), the EUDR was postponed by 12 months to 'allow Member States, exporting partner countries, operators and traders to be better prepared and for the latter, to fully establish the necessary due diligence systems covering all relevant commodities and products'.[31] The EUDR's timeline is presented in the Fig. 3.3.

EUDR's creation divided positionings globally. Some authors[32] view the norm creation favourably, proposing that the EU must use trade regulations to lessen its deforestation footprint. They seek to demonstrate how moral, legal, and pragmatic concerns converge when determining shared responsibility for environmental harm. Other authors[33] criticize the norm, mainly the exclusion of products such as maize, financial institutions, and other ecosystems; the explicitly exclusion of principles of environmental law; and the high cost of compliance with obligations, mainly for local communities, which may significantly increase the value of products.

Further studies delve into the economic impacts of the EUDR globally. For instance, research found out that the introduction of new mandatory due diligence regulations (such as the EUDR) can significantly impact economic actors in developing countries in terms of operation costs, prices, and production volumes, and potentially reduce the benefits derived from international trade.[34] Other studies found

[27] Ibid.

[28] USDA (2020).

[29] EUR-Lex (2024).

[30] Ibid.

[31] European Council (2024a, b).

[32] Marín Durán and Scott (2022, p. 245).

[33] Bertoldi (2024).

[34] UNCTAD (2025).

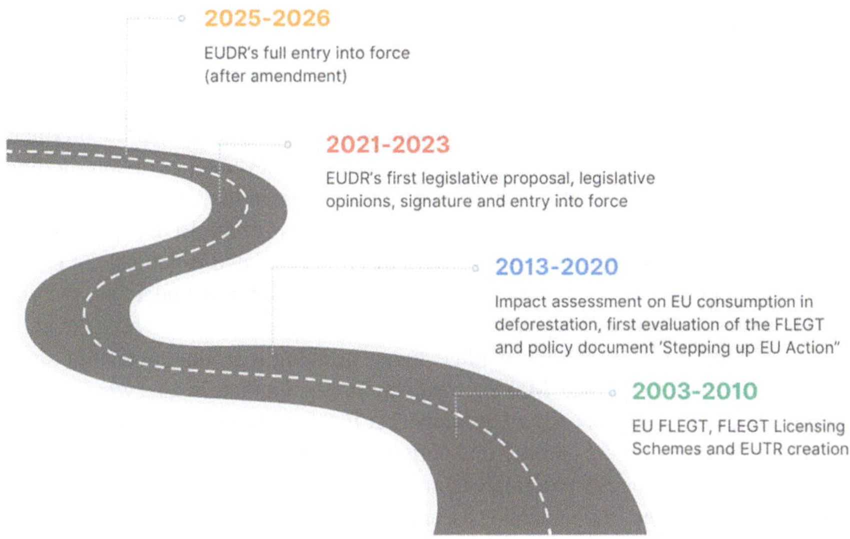

Fig. 3.3. EUDR's timeline

that the EUDR will have a significant impact on some developing country exports,[35] as well it could cost EU consumers up to $1.5 billion.[36] However, there is still no consensus on that matter, as other research shows that the costs generated by EUDR may be minimal.[37]

3.2 EUDR'S Normative Challenges

The EUDR's legal text has several controversial issues concerning requirements, criteria and definitions of the norm, the lack of them or insufficient detail. This may create challenges for EU players and third countries as it prevents a full and clear understanding of the EUDR and its predictability.

This section discusses these challenges under two perspectives: a normative one, by discussing issues related to legal provisions of the EUDR; an operational one, by assessing potential practical bottlenecks derived from the implementation of these provisions.

[35] Arenas and Echandi (2023).

[36] GlobalData (2024).

[37] Kuepper and Rijk (2025).

3.2.1 *Challenges Concerning the Legal Provisions*

The EUDR aims to rule over the 'placing and making available on the Union market as well as the export from the Union of relevant products'.[38] These 'relevant products' are those listed[39] in Annex I of the norm and encompass seven types of commodities (cattle, cocoa, coffee, oil palm, rubber, soya and wood). In the case of products not listed in the current version of the Annex or its updates (as the EUDR provides for periodic revisions[40]), even when they originate from regulated products, the EUDR will not be applicable. The risk of circumvention, however, must be addressed both by authorities and private entities.[41]

As defined,[42] 'placing on the market' means making a product available on the EU market for the first time. 'Making available on the market' means when a trader supplies relevant products on the Union market for distribution, consumption or for use under the course of its commercial activity. Finally, 'export' means any activity of exportation from the EU to abroad. Thus, the EUDR aims to regulate mainly three types of commodities 'movements': its insertion into the EU, its circulation and its export.

The EUDR also highlights other important definitions,[43] such as 'forest'[44]; 'forest degradation'[45]; 'deforestation-free'[46]; 'competent authorities',[47] and 'relevant legislation of the country of production'.[48] Regarding regulated players, the EUDR divides

[38] See Article 1 of the EUDR.

[39] The EUDR provides a list of Harmonised System codes under its scope.

[40] See Article 34 of the EUDR. The EUDR also is expected to repel with effect the EUTR from 30 December 2024, or, in the case of timber and timber products that were produced before 29 June 2023 and placed on the market from 30 December 2024, from 31 December 2027.

[41] See Articles 10.2 (i), 13 and 15 (3) of the EUDR.

[42] See Article 2 of the EUDR.

[43] See Article 2 of the EUDR.

[44] Defined as land spanning more than 0,5 hectares with trees higher than 5 m and a canopy cover of more than 10%, or trees able to reach those thresholds in situ, excluding land that is predominantly under agricultural or urban land use; 'deforestation', that means the conversion of forest to agricultural use, whether human-induced or not.

[45] The structural changes to forest cover, taking the form of the conversion of: (a) primary forests or naturally regenerating forests into plantation forests or into other wooded land; or (b) primary forests into planted forests.

[46] Which means (a), that the relevant products contain, have been fed with or have been made using, relevant commodities that were produced on land that has not been subject to deforestation after 31 December, 2020; and (b), in the case of relevant products that contain or have been made using wood, that the wood has been harvested from the forest without inducing forest degradation after 31 December, 2020.

[47] National entities responsible for fulfilling the obligations arising from the Regulation. Until the end of 2024, not all countries had appointed their list of entities.

[48] Laws applicable in the country of production concerning the legal status of the area of production in terms of: (a), land use rights; (b), environmental protection; (c), forest-related rules, including forest management and biodiversity conservation, where directly related to wood harvesting;

(d), third parties' rights; (e), labour rights; (f), human rights protected under international law;

them into 'operators'[49] and 'traders',[50] where the former has more obligations than the latter.[51]

At a first glance, one might believe that the EUDR may only apply to players (operators and traders) who fall into one of the three stages listed above: when the product is first placed on the EU market, when any other commercial activity is conducted within the market or in the case of an export operation from the EU. However, for the norm to be faithfully complied with, the entire supply chain needs to be adapted.

The EUDR is divided into three requirements[52]: regulated products must be (i) deforestation-free[53]; (ii) produced in accordance with the relevant legislation of the country of production; and (iii) covered by a due diligence statement.[54] Particularly, the two latter affect countries from outside the EU.

These EUDR's requirements are not free from challenges. For instance, the timeframe specification for 'deforestation-free' may be controversial, as it adopts a deforestation-only criterion, excluding, for instance, reforestation policies. The EUDR text also lacks clear provision concerning what it considers time and place of production. This was later addressed in the Guidance, which stated that in most cases it will be 'the time of harvest of the commodity, with the exception of cattle products in which case the relevant time of production starts on the date on which the cattle is born.[55]

Regarding compliance with relevant legislation of the country of production, only the applicable laws concerning the legal status of the area of production shall be considered,[56] such as, inter alia, land use rights, environmental protection, forest-related rules, third parties' rights (including rights to use and tenure affected by producing the relevant commodities and products, and traditional land use rights of indigenous peoples and local communities), labour rights and human rights protected

(g), the principle of free, prior and informed consent (FPIC), including as set out in the UN Declaration on the Rights of Indigenous Peoples; (h), tax, anti-corruption, trade and customs regulations.

[49] As described in the EUDR's Article 2, 'any natural or legal person who, in the course of a commercial activity, places relevant products on the market or exports them'.

[50] As described in the EUDR's Article 2, 'any person in the supply chain other than the operator who, in the course of a commercial activity, makes relevant products available on the market'.

[51] See Articles 4 and 5 of the EUDR.

[52] See Article 3 of the EUDR.

[53] As defined in the EUDR's Article 2, 'deforestation-free' means: (a), that the relevant products contain, have been fed with or have been made using, relevant commodities that were produced on land that has not been subject to deforestation after 31 December, 2020; and (b), in the case of relevant products that contain or have been made using wood, that the wood has been harvested from the forest without inducing forest degradation after 31 December, 2020.

[54] Due diligence statements must include detailed information that proves the products comply with the EUDR; risk assessment for each product, to define the risk of non-compliance, including the establishment of a three-tier benchmark risk system; and, if necessary, risk mitigation measures.

[55] EUR-Lex (2024).

[56] Ibid.

under international law, the principle of free, prior and informed consent, and tax, anti-corruption, trade and customs regulations. As expressed by Sir Nicholas Forwood,[57] this does not limit 'relevant legislation' to those that regulate formal legal interests in land, but extends to any law of the types described above.

Compliance with relevant legislation must be proved within due diligence statements. However, the EUDR text does not specify further requirements for how this information can be provided. For instance, the Guidance[58] issued in November 2024 states that the obligation to collect documents or other information depends on the different regulatory regimes of countries, but will include documents such as administrative permits, contracts and judicial decisions.

Due diligence requirements go further than providing information about the legislation of the country of production. Obligations are divided into three steps[59]: (a) collection of information, data and documents[60]; (b) risk assessment measures[61]; and (c) risk mitigation measures.[62] In order to exercise due diligence, operators must establish and keep up to date a framework of procedures and measures to ensure that their products comply with the EUDR.[63] This information shall be included via Due Diligence Statements (DDS) in the Information System (IS),[64] platform specifically created for the EUDR's operationalization. Figure 3.4 provides a summary of the due diligence requirements under the EUDR.

The IS aims to facilitate the submission and processing of DDS for relevant operators, traders (which are not SME), competent authorities and customs. Operators shall collect, organise and keep for five years the information gathered, accompanied by evidence. Also, the operators should be able to demonstrate how due diligence was carried out and what mitigation measures were put in place in case the risk was identified.

The IS and, subsequently, its interconnection with the EU Single Window Environment for Customs are expected to be aligned with the relevant and applicable provisions in terms of data protection. In line with the EU's Open Data Policy, the European Commission aims to provide access to the wider public to the complete anonymised datasets of the IS in an open format that can be machine-readable and that ensures interoperability, re-use, and accessibility. The System is not free of criticism as stakeholders had pleaded for lifting archives limitation and accepting other data formats than the only GeoJSON standard.[65]

As observed, a major challenge is still the lack of detail regarding criteria for applying the EU and whether documents (even if they comply with the legislation

---

[57] Forwood (2025).

[58] Ibid.

[59] See Article 8 of the EUDR.

[60] See Article 9 of the EUDR.

[61] See Article 10 of the EUDR.

[62] See Article 11 of the EUDR.

[63] See Article 12 of the EUDR.

[64] See Article 33 of the EUDR.

[65] CPDG (2024).

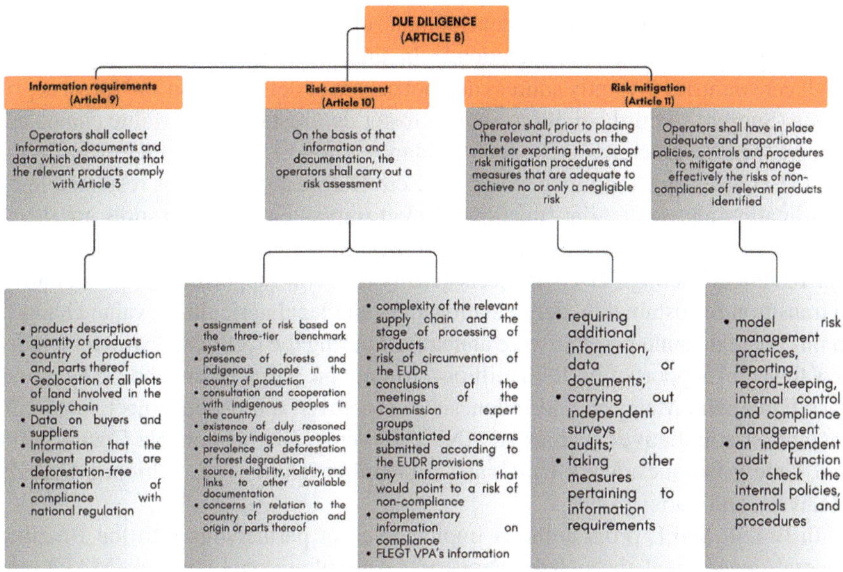

Fig. 3.4 Summary of EUDR's due diligence requirements

of the country of origin) will be accepted. Potentially, the practical interpretation of this will be defined by the competent authorities, the institutions responsible for implementing the standard on a daily basis in the EU.

Each EU Member State must appoint each of its own institutions will act as competent authorities. However, by January 2025, not all countries had actually appointed their respective authorities. Moreover, there is a discrepancy in the scope of these institutions as, for example, there are competent authorities linked to the federal police department, the ministry of the environment or foreign trade. This can potentially lead to divergent interpretations of the EUDR.

The lack of more comprehensive guidance at administrative level in the EU can lead to divergent interpretations and applications of the norm. In fact, if these divergences lead to discrepancies in the application of the EUDR, it is possible that some kind of 'market shopping' could be created, in which EU countries considered less demanding in terms of the application of the EUDR are favoured for the entry of products, thus resulting in potential commercial and infrastructure impacts.

In a non-compliance event, the EUDR provides for both corrective actions[66] and penalties,[67] such as fines, confiscations, temporary exclusion from public procurement processes and from access to public funding and temporary prohibition from placing or making available on the market or exporting relevant commodities and relevant products.

[66] See article 24 of the EUDR.

[67] See article 25 of the EUDR.

The EUDR provides for the development of relationships with third countries through partnerships and cooperation.[68] In this sense, the EU shall engage with producer countries to jointly address the root causes of deforestation and forest degradation. Support to third countries aims to foster deforestation-free value chains and follows specific structures.[69] Strategic guidance is conducted by Team Europe Initiative (TEI) Steering Committee, while the Zero Deforestation Hub is responsible for coordination and secretariat functions. Direct implementation measures are developed by the Sustainable Agriculture for Forest Ecosystems (SAFE) programme[70] and Technical Facility (TF).[71] Projects usually focus on supporting partner countries to transition to sustainable, deforestation-free, and legal agricultural value chains.[72] In this context, some projects were announced during the COP 28,[73] which included new financial support of EUR 70 million[74] to strategic partners; and the Ad Hoc Joint Task Force with Malaysia and Indonesia.[75] Moreover, a broader project ecosystem encompasses initiatives such as AL-INVEST Verde, EU Sustainable Cocoa Initiative, Café y Bosques, Mark Up II, and Bilateral envelopes (e.g. Ethiopia, Uganda, Malaysia, and Laos).

In Brazil, SAFE programme is implemented in partnership with the Brazilian Federal Government, through the Ministry of Agriculture and Livestock (MAPA) and the German development agency Deutsche Gesellschaft für Internationale Zusammenarbeit (GIZ).[76] The project aims to foster the sustainability of cocoa and cattle production chains, regularisation and legality in production, improvement of market access and value addition, traceability systems promotion, incentives for the preservation of forest ecosystems, and access to finance. Activities are concentrated in the pilot area of the Xingu region, in the municipality of Altamira, in the state of Pará, with a focus on local producers.

Relationship with third countries also include a country-risk system (benchmarking).[77] This is a three-tier system for the assessment of countries in risk categories of 'average', 'low' and 'high' risks based on an objective and transparent assessment by the EU Commission, also taking into account the latest scientific evidence and internationally recognised sources. For instance, criteria to be assessed include the rate of deforestation and forest degradation; rate of expansion of agriculture land for relevant commodities; and production trends of relevant commodities and of relevant products.

---

[68] See Article 30 of the EUDR.

[69] European Commission (2025a, b).

[70] The SAFE programme provides long-term support on deforestation-free value chains in partners countries such as Brazil, Ecuador, Indonesia and Vietnam.

[71] The TF provides demand driven support to EUDs and partner countries.

[72] Zero Deforestation Hub (2024).

[73] European Commission (2023).

[74] Ibid.

[75] Ibid.

[76] Zero Deforestation Hub (2025).

[77] See Article 29 of the EUDR. All countries shall be initially classified as 'standard risk'.

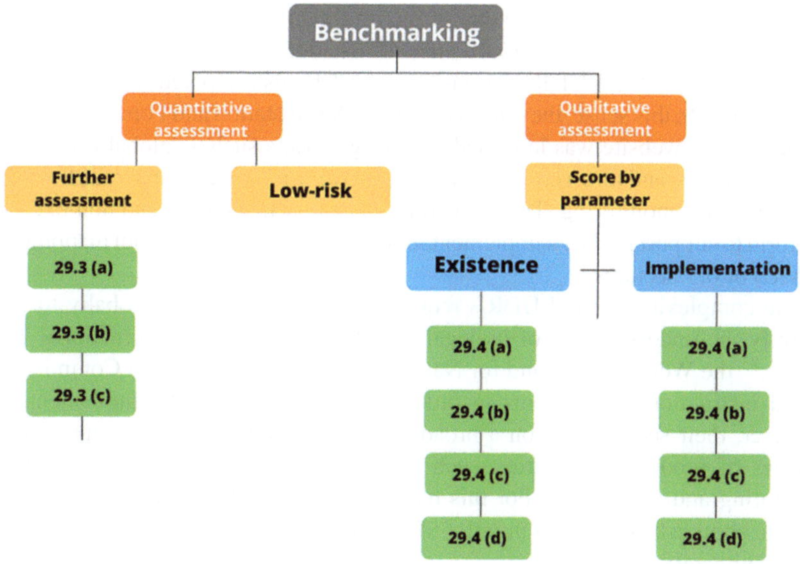

Fig. 3.5 Benchmarking general principles

The benchmarking is extremely relevant, as it will create degrees of enforceability of EUDR requirements based on countries risk assessment. As such, its poor implementation can result in discriminatory application of the EUDR by adopting arbitrary or insufficient criteria for classifying each country. However, up to the end of the original transitional period, there was no benchmarking methodology, which further contributed to delaying EUDR's entry into force.[78] The general principles of benchmarking are summarised in Fig. 3.5.

Aiming to facilitate and guide stakeholders, the European Commission articulated several focal points and supporting documents to address issues related to the EUDR. For instance, the 'European Commission expert group Multi-Stakeholder Platform on Protecting and Restoring the World's Forests'[79] serves as a forum to foster exchanges among stakeholders' participation and is open to all countries. However, in 2024, the UE established a specific Committee to support the EUDR's implementation[80] and to support its development.

Until then, the 'Frequented Asked Questions' (FAQ)[81] document has served as the main focal instrument to resolve any doubts about the norm. However, the FAQ suffered from delays in being updated (with a period of almost a year between the second and third versions) and it was still insufficient regarding some themes as they were not fully (or clearly) addressed. Other supporting documents were overdue

[78] EUR-Lex (2025).

[79] European Union (2024a, b, c, d).

[80] European Union (2024a, b, c, d).

[81] European Commission (2024a, b, c, d, e).

and were only published by the end of the original transitional period, such as the EUDR's Guidance[82] and the first IS manual[83] (and its trainings sessions).

To implement the EUDR's provisions, the EU also adopted some supporting mechanisms. In this sense, the 'Observatory on Deforestation and Forest Degradation Monitoring'[84] website was launched, covering aspects such as global forest cover, forest attributes, and forest cover changes and drivers; production and trade flows; and tools for forest monitoring. The Observatory is a non-mandatory and non-exclusive platform to support EUDR's implementation and considers a minimum mapping area (MMU) of 0,5 hectares.

The complexity of the EUDR's requirements surged players globally to try to simplify the understanding of its legal text. For example, the International Trade Centre,[85] the World Wide Fund for Nature[86] and even the European Commission[87] issued instructional documents in order to clarify the EUDR's implementation. However, their scope focus on a broader approach and do not encompass particularities of producing countries, such as relevant legislation and mechanism for monitoring and traceability. For this reason, as will be developed further, a more specific approach is required in order to fully comprehend potential challenges and opportunities for some country.

3.2.2 Potential Operational Bottlenecks Derived from the EUDR's Implementation

As discussed in the last section, the EUDR requires regulated products to meet three main cumulative obligations: (i) they are deforestation-free; (ii) produced in accordance with the relevant legislation of the country of production; and (iii) covered by a DDS. However, these requirements still lack further guidance and clear definitions, thus preventing some level of predictability concerning the application of the norm and, consequently, halting efforts to comply if it. The primary obligations of the EUDR are schematically represented in Fig. 3.6.

Third countries producers and exporters need to adapt their products and procedures to give inputs to EU importers and other counterparts, thus complying with the EUDR. If they fail to do so, or even demonstrate a possible risk of non-compliance, EU players may cease purchases or even terminate contracts. Understanding all aspects of an operational chain is required to both identify potential bottlenecks and properly address these issues.

[82] EUR-Lex (2024).

[83] European Union (2024a, b, c, d).

[84] European Union, (2024a, b, c, d).

[85] International Trade Centre (2024).

[86] WWF (2024a, b).

[87] European Commission: Directorate-General for Environment (2025).

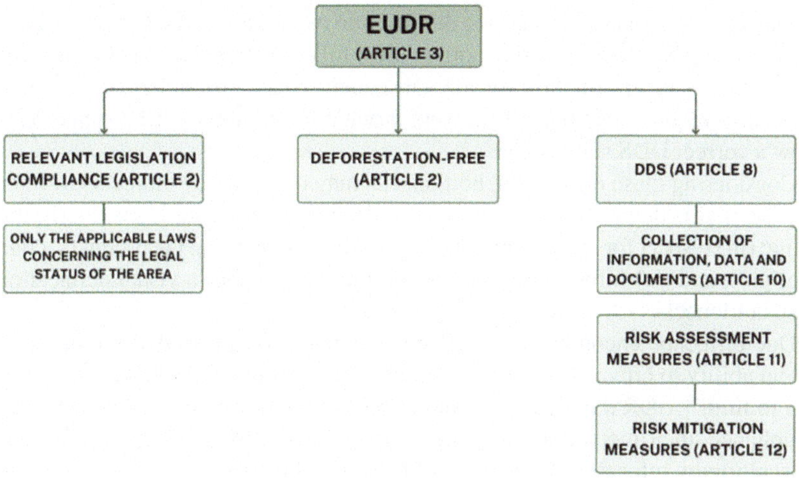

Fig. 3.6 EUDR's main obligations

Operations between a third country and the EU often take form in a similar way. First steps usually come within the commodity producer's country. Generally, producers have three main options to place its products on the EU market: (i) they can deal directly with an EU buyer (operator); (ii) hire an intermediary (such as a cooperative, broker or association); or (iii) use a trading company to operationalise the sale to the EU. In all cases, players need to ensure compliance with the EUDR to guarantee the conformity and viability of the operation. Figure 3.7 presents an overview of third countries-EU operations.

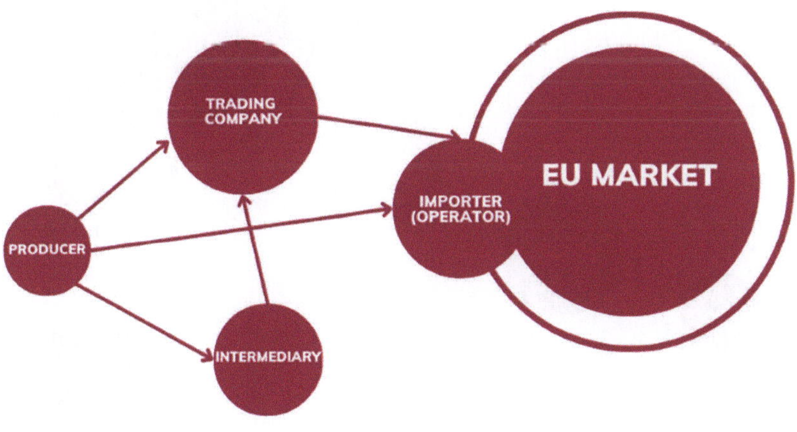

Fig. 3.7 Overview of third countries-EU operations

These types of operations may be divided into two main phases. Firstly, a 'national phase' in which producers and exporters must follow national legislation and obtain all the necessary information for the subsequent phase. Secondly, an 'EU phase', which also requires that non-EU players provide information to EU counterparts to allow a correct DDS submission.

Considering these operations, bottlenecks may occur at key moments of interaction. We divide them in four groups: (i) due diligence (in a generic sense); (ii) monitoring; (iii) respect for relevant national legislation (concerning the products' country of origin); and (iv) Information System. Figure 3.8 provides a visual delineation of these bottlenecks.

Due diligence encompasses a full understanding of the EUDR's requirements and an ability to effectively conduct activities to meet them. As players may not be able to fulfil EUDR's obligations—either because they lack mechanisms to certify compliance, their methodology is not compatible with the EU's system or there is a discretionary refusal on the part of competent authorities or EU buyers—conflicts may arise along the entire value chain.

Monitoring concerns the identification and collection of the most important information and which instruments to use for this. This is a step majorly related to producers as they must guarantee their products are deforestation-free in accordance with the EUDR. Without effective monitoring mechanisms, it is not possible

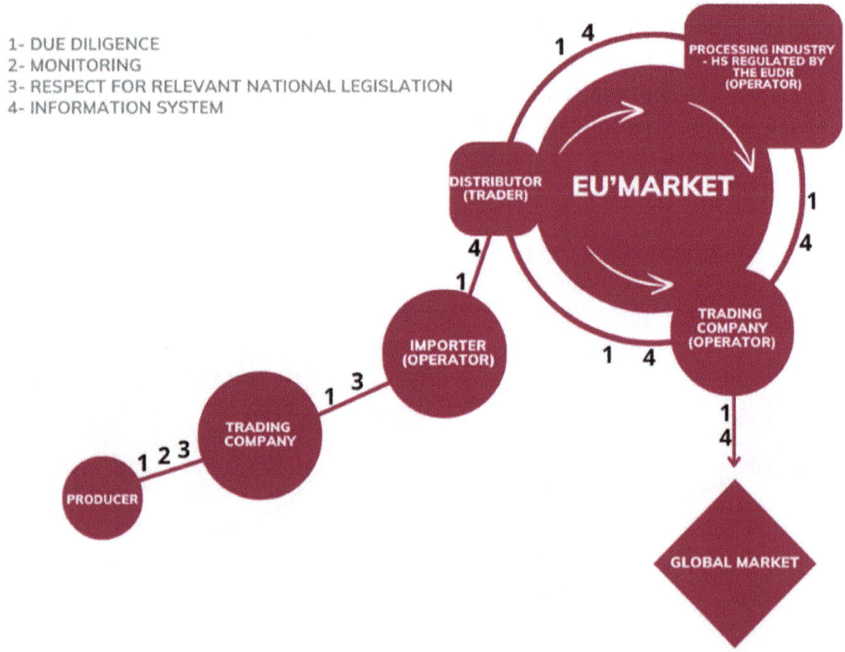

Fig. 3.8 General EUDR bottlenecks

to provide required information when submitting DDS, thus making the operation non-compliant to the EUDR.

Respect for relevant national legislation comprises the identification of which norms must be complied with and what documents are necessary to attest to this conformity. This encompasses the entire national phase. As in the case of monitoring challenges, if players cannot attest their compliance with national norms or EU authorities and buyers do not recognize it, products shall not to be placed on the EU market.

Lastly, Information System relates to both the IS per se (as a technical system) and information channels between producers and exporters and their EU counterparts. This encompasses majorly the EU phase, specifically during and after placing the product in the market. Players must ensure that information flows along their entire value chain, guaranteeing that all data is provided by the time of DDS submission.

3.2.3 Reactions

As mentioned before, the EU's stance on deforestation through product regulations has faced both praise and criticism worldwide, creating a complex and sometimes contradictory landscape of international responses. Reactions came at different levels, including at the WTO and its CTE, unilaterally by countries, by group of countries or associations.

At the WTO, some producing countries have warned of potential economic fallout from the EUDR, raising concerns about their commodity exports. As mentioned, in November 2022, representatives from 17 countries, including major exporters like Brazil and Indonesia, raised objections to the EUDR in a letter to EU officials.[88] Later, representatives from both Latin and Central American exporting countries have raised concerns with the WTO regarding potential negative effects of the EUDR.[89]

Particularly, the EUDR has sparked mixed reactions within Brazil's economic community, with some stakeholders expressing apprehension about its potential effects. The Brazilian National Confederation of Industry (CNI) expressed its concerned about the approval of the EUDR, as it could create disproportionate barriers to international trade and negatively impact the Brazilian agro-industrial sector.[90] The Brazilian Agribusiness Association (ABAG) has also criticized the EUDR, stating that it fails to recognize the Brazilian Forest Code, which authorizes legal deforestation in designated areas of rural properties.[91]

Other exporting countries such as Indonesia have criticized the EUDR, claiming it unfairly disadvantages its palm oil producers in international markets and lacks

[88] World Trade Organization (2022).

[89] World Trade Organization, WT/GC/W912 (2022).

[90] Confederação Nacional de Indústrias (2023).

[91] ABAG (2023).

support for compliance.[92] They argue the EUDR ignores Indonesia's considerable progress in tackling palm oil deforestation and warn it could even incentivize further deforestation due to potential market segregation.

Later, on 8 March 2024, the United States issued a letter to EU's Ambassador Katherine Tai addressing possible impacts of the EUDR in the US.[93] Also, on 21 March 2024, a note[94] from the Austrian delegation supported by the Finish, Italian, Polish, Slovak, Slovenian, and Swedish delegations called for 'urgent' action in the face of the EUDR' implementation due to imminent negative effects on sustainable and small-scale agricultural and forestry practices in the EU.

From the point of view of civil society, reactions have also been mixed. On the one hand, some groups have expressed concerns regarding the EUDR. For instance, on 28 March 2024, a group of associations of producers addressed a joint cross-commodity[95] call to the EU Commission and Member States to provide urgent clarifications and workable solutions for EUDR implementation. On 8 April 2024, global forest-based industries' called for legal clarity and adequate transition time to ensure a 'smooth and effective' implementation of the EUDR.[96]

On the other hand, different organizations praised the EUDR and signalled support for its implementation. On December 2023, a joint letter of civil society organisations[97] working in non-EU countries expressed appreciation for the EUDR as an initiative that helps tackling the global biodiversity and climate crisis. Later on March 2024, World Wildlife Fund organization issued a document entitled 'No Ecosystem Left Behind' [98] supporting the EUDR's and calling for changes in its definition of forests in order to include other biomes, such as the Cerrado in Brazil. On 11 April 2024, over 100 entities from the civil society signed a letter to reiterate their full support for the EUDR. On May 15, 2024, 25 Brazilian institutions addressed a letter[99] to the European Commission claiming that postponing EUDR could discredit EU commitments to fighting climate change and biodiversity loss. Lastly, on 17 May 2024, associations from different commodities sectors stated their commitment and need for a successful implementation of the EUDR, also highlighting some technical challenges in order to do so.[100]

The EUDR-related themes also sparked debate on several policy measures worldwide. For instance, Brazil[101] is discussing potential 'reciprocity' act in order to adopt trade countermeasures in response to unilateral actions by countries or economic blocs that harm the country's international competitiveness. Moreover,

[92] Reuters (2023).

[93] Unites States Senate (2024).

[94] Council of the European Union (2024a, b, c, d).

[95] EU cross-commodity coalition on EUDR implementation (2024).

[96] AF&PA et al. (2024).

[97] Amigos da Terra et al. (2023).

[98] WWF (2024a, b).

[99] APIB et al. (2024).

[100] Bioenergy Europe et al. (2024).

[101] Senado (2025).

United Kingdom,[102] United States[103] and Thailand[104] are developing their own deforestation-free regulations.

Considering these, several countries conducted dry runs in order to assess preparation level and potential bottlenecks related to the EUDR operationalization. For instance, Mercosur's countries found some difficulties—and uncertainty—in fully complying with EUDR's information requirements[105] in beef and soy sectors.

Due to the various criticisms and the lack of documents and mechanisms provided by the EUDR's text, the European Commission proposed a one-year delay of the norm, which was then approved by December 2024. The decision to postpone the entry into force of the EUDR has been also met with a mixed response from various sectors of society. While a number of organizations have criticized the postponement,[106] citing the role of the agricultural lobby, third countries to the EU and companies have welcomed the decision.[107] However, the postponement has given stakeholders and the EU itself more time to address criticized key topics.

3.3 Section Conclusion

Considering this Chapter analysis, several challenges were identified concerning the EUDR's legal text, thus demonstrating some potential bottlenecks to be faced globally. A major challenge is the need of the EU to further specify some of the EUDR definitions, requirements and criteria. Without this, players will lack predictability concerning the application of the norm and will not be able to adapt to its requirements. This may be the source of most identified bottleneck, as the legal text and its interpretation are the basis for an effective operationalization of the norm.

Further interpretation of the EUDR could be provided by other legal documents or, in a complementary manner, supporting documents. Yet, the EUDR's implementation has faced challenges in keeping to its schedule. As for the time of this Book, the lack of a benchmarking methodology is the most critical point to be addressed as it will define the methodology to assess a country risk of no compliance. This also highlights the need to improve dialogues with partners and players from both inside and outside the EU, thus fostering knowledge sharing and addressing effectively key points regarding these bottlenecks.

[102] United Kingdom National Archives (2021).

[103] United States Congress (2023).

[104] Walk Free (2025).

[105] Proforest (2025).

[106] Bataier (2024).

[107] Caobisco (2024).

References

AF&PA et al (2024) Global forest-based industries' call for legal clarity and adequate transition time to ensure a smooth and effective implementation of the EU Deforestation Regulation. https://d4d14e3d-083d-4afc-807e-788bd740bca8.filesusr.com/ugd/d13736_babe73c14ca74f3ab46b98dbd0cbdaf8.pdf. Accessed December 22 2024

Amigos da Terra et al (2023) Joint letter of civil society organisations working in non-EU countries. https://amigosdaterra.org.br/wp-content/uploads/2023/12/Joint-letter-EUDR-12.12.NEW-1.pdf. Accessed December 22 2024

APIB et al (2024) Every second counts to protect global forests and ecosystems. https://www.oc.eco.br/wp-content/uploads/2024/05/Every-second-counts-Letter-to-UVDL-on-EUDR.pdf. Accessed December 22, 2024

Arenas G, Echandi R (2023) Trade and development chart: impact of the EU deforestation regulation. https://blogs.worldbank.org/en/trade/trade-and-development-chart-impact-eu-deforestation-regulation. Accessed 06 Jun 2024

Associação Brasileira do Agronegócio [ABAG] (2023) Associação de agronegócio do Brasil reage contra lei da UE sobre desmatamento. https://abag.com.br/associacao-de-agronegocio-do-brasil-reage-contra-lei-da-ue-sobre-desmatamento/. Accessed December 22 2024

Bataier C (2024) Organizations criticize the postponement of the EU anti-deforestation law and mention agribusiness lobby

Bertoldi M (2024) Understanding the deforestation initiative for European trade in products from the Brazilian Amazon. In: Eritja MC, Fernández-Pons X (eds) (2024) Deploying the European green deal: protecting the environment beyond the EU borders, 1st edn. Routledge. https://doi-org.peacepalace.idm.oclc.org/10.4324/9781003390510

Bioenergy Europe et al (2024) EUDR information system not yet on track to meet requirements of properly functioning supply chains. https://fefac.eu/newsroom/news/eudr-information-system-not-yet-on-track-to-meet-requirements-of-properly-functioning-supply-chains/. Accessed December 22 2024

Biscosi M (2025) From natura to nature restoration. The ecological objective of the green deal at the legal litmus test. In: Chiti E, Giorgi A (eds) (2025) Ecological sustainability and the law: the European green deal and the new frontiers of sustainability, 1st edn. Routledge. https://doi-org.peacepalace.idm.oclc.org/10.4324/9781003565185

Buysing Damsté C et al (2024) How the EU's green deal is driving business reinvention. https://www.pwc.com/gx/en/issues/esg/eu-green-deal-reinvention.html. Accessed 22 Dec 2024

Caobisco (2024) CAOBISCO statement on the postponement of the EUDR date of application. https://caobisco.eu/caobisco-statement-on-the-postponement-of-the-eudr-date-of-application/. Accessed 16 Jan 2025

Confederação Nacional da Indústria. (2023) Regulamento da União Europeia condiciona importação de determinadas commodities agrícolas e seus derivados a due diligence de desmatamento (Política Comercial n.º 10, 2023). https://static.portaldaindustria.com.br/media/filer_public/78/99/78990af4-d034-4897-8013-252abe5b3ec2/apc_regulamento_ue_desmatamento_ano_2_n_10.pdf. Accessed December 22 2024

CPDG (2024) The EUDR's information system: roadmap and challenges. chrome-extension://efaidnbmnnnibpcajpcglclefindmkaj/https://d4d14e3d-083d-4afc-807e-788bd740bca8.filesusr.com/ugd/d13736_6f552df64a094e599d539ac740019e1e.pdf. Accessed 09 Dec 2024

Earthsight (2025) Blood-stained birch: exposing the EU trade. https://www.earthsight.org.uk/blood-stained-birch. Accessed 16 Mar 2025

EUR-Lex (2010) Regulation (EU) No 995/2010 of the European parliament and of the council of 20 October 2010 laying down the obligations of operators who place timber and timber products on the market. https://eur-lex.europa.eu/eli/reg/2010/995/oj/eng. Accessed 22 Dec 2024

EUR-Lex (2005) Council regulation (EC) No 2173/2005 of 20 December 2005 on the establishment of a FLEGT licensing scheme for imports of timber into the European community. https://eur-lex.europa.eu/eli/reg/2005/2173/oj/eng. Accessed 22 Dec 2024

EUR-Lex (2021a) Procedure 2021/0366/COD. https://eur-lex.europa.eu/legal-content/EN/HIS/?uri=CELEX:32023R1115. Accessed 7 Oct 2024
EUR-Lex (2021b) Regulation (EU) 2021/1119 of the European parliament and of the council of 30 June 2021 establishing the framework for achieving climate neutrality and amending regulations (EC) No 401/2009 and (EU) 2018/1999. https://eur-lex.europa.eu/legal-content/EN/TXT/?uri=CELEX:32021R1119. Accessed 22 Dec 2024
EUR-Lex (2024) Commission notice—guidance document for regulation (EU) 2023/1115 on deforestation-free products. https://eur-lex.europa.eu/legal-content/EN/TXT/?uri=CELEX%3A52024XC06789&qid=1731687748447. Accessed 06 Dec 2024
EUR-Lex. (2025). Communication from the Commission on the Strategic Framework for International Cooperation Engagement in the context of Regulation (EU) 2023/1115 on the making available on the Union market and the export from the Union of certain commodities and products associated with deforestation and forest degradation. https://eur-lex.europa.eu/legal-content/EN/TXT/?uri=CELEX%3A52024XC06604&qid=1731330497871. Accessed 29 May 2025
European Commission (2024) Circular economy action plan. https://environment.ec.europa.eu/strategy/circular-economy-action-plan_en. Accessed 22 Dec 2024
European Commission (2024) Delivering the European green deal: JRC study finds mixed progress so far. https://joint-research-centre.ec.europa.eu/jrc-news-and-updates/delivering-european-green-deal-jrc-study-finds-mixed-progress-so-far-2025-02-05_en. Accessed 11 Feb 2025
European Commission (2021) EU biodiversity strategy for 2030' (2021). https://eur-lex.europa.eu/resource.html?uri=cellar:a3c806a6-9ab3-11ea-9d2d-01aa75ed71a1.0001.02/DOC_1&format=PDF. Accessed 22 Dec 2024
European Commission: Directorate-General for Environment, EUDR compliance (2025) Understanding your position in beef, cocoa, coffee, palm oil, rubber, soy, and wood supply chains, publications office of the European Union. https://data.europa.eu/doi/10.2779/4084343. Accessed 15 Mar 2025
European Union (2024) CIRCABC. https://circabc.europa.eu/ui/welcome. Accessed 22 Dec 2024
European Union (2024) Commission expert group/multi-stakeholder platform on protecting and restoring the world's forests, including the EU timber regulation and the FLEGT regulation' register of commission expert groups and other similar entities. https://ec.europa.eu/transparency/expert-groups-register/screen/home?lang=en. Accessed 28 May 2025
European Union (2024) EU observatory on deforestation and forest degradation. https://forest-observatory.ec.europa.eu/. Accessed 22 Feb 2024
European Commission (2023) COP28: EU steps up cooperation with partner countries on deforestation-free supply outlines further support measures. https://environment.ec.europa.eu/news/cop28-eu-steps-cooperation-partner-countries-deforestation-free-supplychains-and-outlines-further-2023-12-12_en. Accessed 22 Feb 2024
European Commission (2025) EU sanctions alert: high risk of circumvention—import of plywood. https://finance.ec.europa.eu/publications/eu-sanctions-alert-high-risk-circumvention-import-plywood_en. Accessed 19 Mar 2025
European Commission (2024) Frequently asked questions—deforestation regulation. https://environment.ec.europa.eu/publications/frequently-asked-questions-deforestation-regulation_en. Accessed 29 May 2025
European Commission (2024) Nature restoration law. https://environment.ec.europa.eu/topics/nature-and-biodiversity/nature-restoration-law_en. Accessed 22 Dec 2024
European Commission (2025) Team Europe initiative on deforestation-free value chains. https://ec.europa.eu/transparency/expert-groups-register/screen/meetings/consult?lang=en&meetingId=60742&fromExpertGroups=3282. Accessed 15 Mar 2025
European Union (2024) The European union (EU) deforestation-free regulation (EUDR) committee. https://ec.europa.eu/transparency/comitology-register/screen/committees/C128600/consult?lang=en. Accessed 19 Jun 2024

European Commission. (2019). The European green deal (Communication). https://eur-lex.europa.eu/legal-content/EN/TXT/?uri=COM%3A2019%3A640%3AFIN. Accessed 22 Dec 2024
European Council (2024) EU deforestation law: council and parliament agree on its targeted amendment'. https://www.consilium.europa.eu/en/press/press-releases/2024/12/03/eu-deforestation-law-council-and-parliament-agree-on-its-targeted-amendment/. Accessed 22 Dec 2024
European Commission (2024) EU-Mercosur: text of the agreement. https://policy.trade.ec.europa.eu/eu-trade-relationships-country-and-region/countriesand-regions/mercosur/eu-mercosur-agreement/text-agreement_en. Accessed 06 Dec 2024
European Council (2024) European green deal. https://www.consilium.europa.eu/en/policies/green-deal/. Accessed 22 Dec 2024
European Parliament (2019) EU legal framework to halt and reverse EU-driven global deforestation. chrome-extension://efaidnbmnnnibpcajpcglclefindmkaj/https://www.europarl.europa.eu/RegData/etudes/BRIE/2020/658207/IPOL_BRI(2020)658207_EN.pdf. Accessed 7 Oct 2024
EU Cross-Commodity Coalition on EUDR Implementation (2024) Joint cross-commodity call to EU commission and member states to provide urgent clarifications and workable solutions for EUDR implementation. https://www.coceral.com/data/1711704766President%20Khattabi-Joint%20cross%20sector%20coalition%20letter%20on%20EUDR%20implementation.pdf. Accessed December 22 2024
FLEGT License (2025) Indonesian FLEGT licensing procedures. https://flegtlicence.org/www.flegtlicence.org/th/indonesian-flegt-licensing-procedures.html. Accessed 05 Jan 2025
Forwood N (2025) Expert opinion of Sir Nicholas Forwood KC. on the interpretation of articles 2(4) and 3(b) of Regulation (EU) 2023/1115 of the European parliament and council. https://cejmfgv.wixsite.com/website-2/news Accessed 01 Mar 2025
Gheuens J (2023) The European green deal shifting the EU's gaze towards the future?' In: Dyrhauge H, Kurze K (eds) (2023) Making the European green deal work: EU sustainability policies at home and abroad, 1st edn. Routledge. https://doi-org.peacepalace.idm.oclc.org/10.4324/9781003246985
GlobalData (2024) EUDR could cost EU consumers up to $1.5 billion, as new sustainability rules set to impact global commodity supply chains, says new GlobalData study. https://www.globaldata.com/custom-solutions/solutions-in-action/eudr-cost-eu-consumers-1-5-billion-new-sustainability-rules-set-impact-global-commodity-supply-chains-says-new-study/? Accessed 22 Dec 2024
International Trade Centre (2024) New step-by-step guide on EUDR. https://www.intracen.org/news-and-events/news/new-step-by-step-guide-on-eudr. Accessed 22 Feb 2025
Kuepper B, Rijk G (2025) Analysis of EUDR compliance costs. https://profundo.nl/projects/analysis-of-eudr-compliance-costs-/. Accessed 13 Feb 2025
Malingre, V. (2024). Europe's green deal is attacked on all sides', Le monde. https://www.lemonde.fr/en/environment/article/2024/01/29/europe-s-green-deal-is-attacked-on-all-sides_6474382_114.html. Accessed 20 Jun 2024
Marín Durán G, Scott J (2022) Regulating trade in forest-risk commodities: two cheers for the European union' (2022). J Environ Law 34(2):245–267
Proforest (2025) Webinar EUDR–Dry runs for beef and soy supply chains in four Mercosur countries. https://www.youtube.com/watch?v=-Q6W9mtHs60. Accessed March 22 2025
Reuters (2023) COP 28 a global forest fund. https://www.reuters.com/business/environment/brazil-proposes-global-forest-conservationfund-cop28-2023-12-01/. Accessed 22 Feb 2024
Ross J (2024) Court rules Bezos' Superyacht is fitted bow to stern with illegal teak. https://woodcentral.com.au/court-rules-bezos-superyacht-is-fitted-bow-to-stern-with-illegal-teak/. Accessed 02 Jan 2025
Sabillo K (2024) Yacht maker Sunseeker fined in landmark Myanmar 'blood timber' case. https://news.mongabay.com/short-article/yacht-maker-sunseeker-fined-in-landmark-myanmar-blood-timber-case/. Accessed 05 Jan 2025

Senado (2025) Senado aprova Lei da Reciprocidade Econômica. https://www12.senado.leg.br/institucional/presidencia/noticia/davi-alcolumbre/senado-aprova-lei-da-reciprocidade-economica-1. Accessed April 1 2025

UNCTAD (2025) The future of sustainable trade. https://unctad.org/publication/future-sustainable-trade. Accessed 19 Jan 2025

United Kingdom National Archives (2021) Environment Act 2021. https://www.legislation.gov.uk/ukpga/2021/30/enacted

United States Congress (2023) S.3371—118th Congress (2023–2024). https://www.congress.gov/bill/118th-congress/senate-bill/3371/text. Accessed 30 2024

Unites States Senate (2024) March 8, 2024 letter to Ambassador Katherine Tai. chrome-extension://efaidnbmnnnibpcajpcglclefindmkaj/https://www.scott.senate.gov/wp-content/uploads/Senate-Letter-to-USTR-re-EUDR.pdf. Accessed 22 Dec 2024

USDA (2020) EU launches public consultation on deforestation-free supply chains. chrome-extension://efaidnbmnnnibpcajpcglclefindmkaj/https://apps.fas.usda.gov/newgainapi/api/Report/DownloadReportByFileName?fileName=EU%20Launches%20Public%20Consultation%20on%20Deforestation-Free%20Supply%20Chains%20_Brussels%20USEU_European%20Union_09-23-2020. Accessed 17 Dec 2023

Walk Free (2025) Thailand to introduce mandatory supply chain due diligence law. https://www.walkfree.org/news/2025/thailand-to-introduce-mandatory-supply-chain-due-diligence-law/. Accessed March 15 2025

World Trade Organization (2022) Committee on agriculture. Joint letter submitted by Indonesia and Brazil, 29 November 2022. https://docs.wto.org/dol2fe/Pages/SS/directdoc.aspx?filename=q:/G/AG/GEN213.pdf&Open=True. Accessed 22 Dec 2024

WWF (2024) No ecosystem left behind. https://www.wwf.org.br/nossosconteudos/biomas/cerrado/ecosystem/. Accessed 22 Dec 2024

WWF (2024) WWF launches EUDR Step-by-step guide for business. https://forestsforward.panda.org/?14709791/WWF-launches-EUDR-guide-for-business. Accessed 29 May 2025

Zero Deforestation Hub (2024) Team Europe initiative on deforestation-free value chains. https://zerodeforestationhub.eu/. Accessed 29 May 2025

Zero Deforestation Hub (2025) Sustainable agriculture for forest ecosystems [Brazil]. https://zerodeforestationhub.eu/projects/safe/brazil/ Accessed 13 Mar 2025

Chapter 4
Potential Dispute Resolution Alternatives

4.1 Multilateral Trade-Related Disputes

The EUDR is a market-based measure that aims to affect GHG emissions by regulating economic dynamics. In this sense, and considering the bottlenecks highlighted in the previous chapter, the norm can potentially have implications for commercial relations between EU and third countries players. If the EUDR is not properly implemented (nor operationalized by players), this could foster conflicts between parties within a value chain.

4.1.1 Potential Impact on Trade Flux

As observed in the previous chapter, several studies found the EUDR's potential impacts on the international trade flux. This is particularly true to producing countries depended on the export of its products. As stated in the UN Trade and Development's State of Commodity Dependence 2021 report,[1] more than 100 countries were dependent on commodity exports. Several studies have also tried to assess potential economic impacts of the EUDR. While some works assessed high cost for

[1] United Nations Trade and Development (2021).

Pedro Henrique Lavinas Ortman, researcher at FGV Rio Law's Jean Monnet Centre of Excellence on EU-LA Global Challenges, co-funded by the European Commission, and the Centre for Global Law, is a contributing author to subsection "Alternative dispute resolution mechanisms" in this chapter.

P. Wojcikiewicz Almeida et al., *The Normative and Regulatory Challenges for the Implementation of the European Deforestation-Free Regulation in Third Affected Countries*, https://doi.org/10.1007/978-3-032-08458-3_4

Table 4.1 Brazilian agro-based products exports

(USD million)	2018	2019	2020	2021
Agri-business exports	101,167	96,851	100,702	120,521
Agri-business imports	14,038	13,769	13,047	15,528
Agri-business trade balance	87,130	83,082	87,655	104,993
Total trade balance	58,033	48,036	50,941	61,407

consumers,[2] other studies found minimal impacts.[3] Also, more specific research[4] found that high-deforestation countries are expected to face significant reductions in roundwood production and exports, as well as potential for market leakage.

Disruptions in value chains can generate profound socio-economic impacts in these nations. According to the WTO,[5] Brazil has a huge dependence on commodities exports, as it is a major player in the global trade of certain agricultural commodities such as soybeans, beef, poultry meat, sugar, orange juice, and coffee. Table 4.1 shows Brazilian exports of agro-based products.

EUDR's commodities exports are usually concentrated in America (particularly, Brazil, Mexico and United States), Europe, Asia and some countries form Africa. Considering commodity-dependence, a focus on a single target market may represent potentials risks to value chains. This is especially true to small and medium-sized producers as they are among the most vulnerable groups. Smallholders may fear the EUDR could burden them with high costs and exclude them from key markets, potentially driving them towards unsustainable practices due to limited alternatives. Additionally, bigger companies, facing new regulations, may simplify supply chains by excluding smallholders who struggle with implementing traceability systems. Exports of EUDR's regulated commodities by origin in 2022 may be observed in Fig. 4.1.

[2] GlobalData (2024).

[3] Profundo (2025).

[4] Johnston et al. (2025).

[5] World Trade Organization (2022a).

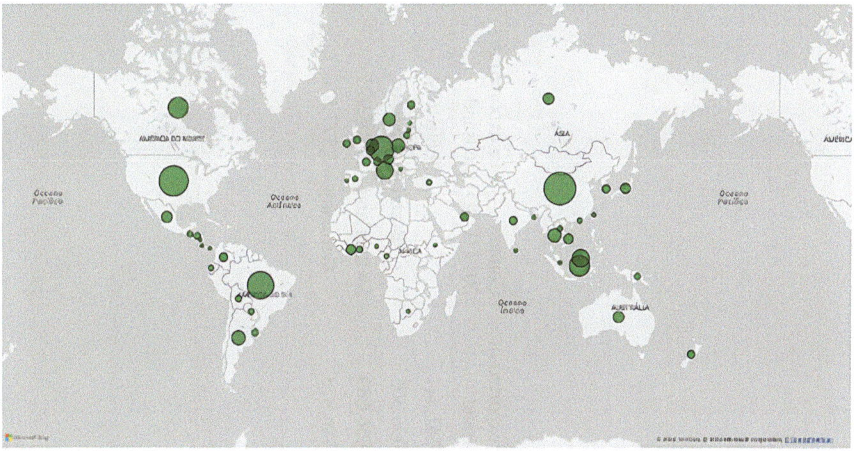

Fig. 4.1 Exports by origin of EUDR's regulated commodities in 2022 (based on ITC data[6])

For instance, the international coffee market is dominated manly by four countries: Brazil, Colombia, Switzerland and Germany. Brazil tops coffee exports, and nearly half of it goes to the EU.[7] On the other hand, Brazil imports from the EU industrialized products of these same goods,[8] thus generating an asymmetry in the trade balance. Table 4.2 illustrates the value of coffee exported worldwide.

Despite the EU ensuring that the EUDR will not cause trade disruptions in the international system,[9] studies seen to find the opposite. The World Bank, for instance, found that it is likely to affect low- and middle-income exporters of cattle, cocoa, coffee, palm oil, rubber, soy, and wood.[10] Other research also found impacts on the exports of great economies, such as the United States[11] and China.[12]

Literature also finds that regulations burden international trade, which also represents potential negative impacts to buyers.[13] Particularly, the increase of EU environmental regulation based on market access may cause increased regulatory uncertainty for companies as businesses will find it difficult to ensure compliance with complex comprehensive norms.[14]

As the EUDR will potentially affect both supply and demand sides of international trade, concerns regarding its compliance vis-à-vis the international trade regime are urging countries to contest the EUDR at the WTO.

---

[6] International Trade Centre (2024).

[7] Brazil Comexstat (2024).

[8] Brazil Comexstat (2024).

[9] European Commission (2024b).

[10] Sikora and Sela (2024).

[11] Congressional Research Service (2024).

[12] WWF (2024a).

[13] Nabeshima and Obashi (2021, p. 59).

[14] Kommerkollegium (2024).

Table 4.2 Value of coffee exported worldwide (2019–2022)

Exporters	Country—Value exported in 2022 (USD) thousand	Country—Value exported in 2021 (USD) thousand	Country—Value exported in 2020 (USD) thousand	Country—Value exported in 2019 (USD) thousand
World	43,356,192	36,383,423	30,742,341	29,601,674
1st biggest exporter	Brazil—8,542,533	Brazil—5,833,257	Brazil—4,996,305	Brazil—4,553,569
2nd biggest exporter	Colombia—4,108,629	Switzerland—3,601,361	Switzerland—2,856,689	Switzerland—2,508,925
3rd biggest exporter	Switzerland—3,422,252	Colombia—3,188,816	Germany—2,586,875	Germany—2,377,576

4.1.2 Contestation at the WTO

Current multilateral trade regime is based on the foundation of the WTO. As there is mixed reception to the EUDR worldwide, as well as considering potential impacts on the international trade flux, potential litigation may be brought to Organization. As the norm is not yet full into force, it still not possible to precisely determine potential dispute scenarios. However, current negative reactions worldwide, claims of violation son international trade law and bottlenecks that are beginning to form between contractual parties are already leading to potential points of conflict in the near future.

For instance, in November 2022 representatives from 17 countries, including major exporters like Brazil and Indonesia, raised objections to the EUDR in a letter to EU officials expressing concerns about potential discrimination, WTO compliance, and impacts on small businesses, urging changes and open dialogue.[15] Later, representatives from both Latin and Central American exporting countries also raised concerns with the WTO regarding potential negative effects of the EUDR.[16] Therefore, the WTO will potentially (if not probably) be used as a forum to settle disputes originated form the implementation of the EUDR.

Before the WTO system, the greatest milestone on international trade regime was the signature of the General Agreement on Tariffs and Trade (GATT) in 1947. Despite the predominance of an economic approach, the multilateral trade regime aimed to cover a broad range of topics, which can be seen by the GATT's introduction of environmental issues into its own agenda.[17]

Later in 1994, the Marrakesh Agreement (WTO Agreement) finally gave birth to the WTO as we have today. In the Agreement's Preamble, it further expanded its scope to the environmental agenda by acknowledging the importance of the optimal use of the world's resources in accordance with the objective of sustainable development, aiming to protect and preserve the environment while addressing the diverse needs and concerns at various stages of development.[18] Furthermore, the newfound organization began to establish other mechanisms to specifically address environment-related issues, such as[19]:

(i) The Agreement on Technical Barriers to Trade (TBT), which provides for technical and regulatory standards, as well as assessment procedures for trade;
(ii) The Agreement on Sanitary and Phytosanitary Standards (SPS), that lays down stringent standards for making rules governing sanitary and phytosanitary measures; and

[15] WTO Committee on Agriculture (2022b).

[16] World Trade Organization (2023a).

[17] Charnovitz (1997) and World Trade Organization (2004).

[18] World Trade Organization Marrakesh Agreement (1994).

[19] Shukla (2024, pp. 115–130).

(iii) The Committee on Trade and Environment (CTE), that aims to provide recommendations to bring environmental concerns withing WTO's policy setup.

Currently, as the nexus between trade-environment grew stronger,[20] nearly all WTO Agreements include provisions addressing environmental concerns. In fact, the annual rate of environment-related notifications in the Organization rose more than four times from 1997 to 2022.[21]

When an infringement occurs under the WTO framework, including in relation to environmental issues, the Dispute Settlement Body[22] (DSB) is up to rule over litigation cases. The DSB consists of all WTO members and has the sole authority to establish 'panels' of experts to consider the case, and to accept or reject the panels' findings or the results of an appeal. It also monitors the implementation of the rulings and recommendations, and can authorize retaliation when a country does not comply with a ruling.

Procedure under the DSB is divided mainly in two stages. Firstly, there is a consultation stage, which may take up to 60 days. Member states are required to engage in consultations, mediation, and other forms of dispute settlement[23] before resorting to the formal two-tiered process outlined in the DSU. Article 5 of the DSU specifically mentions conciliation, alongside good offices and mediation, as a voluntary and confidential way to resolve disputes. It can be used at any time, ideally before the panel process but even during it. The DSU rules further emphasize conciliation by empowering the Director-General to offer these services to disputing parties. Despite its prominent position in the DSU, conciliation is reportedly underutilized in practice.

Then, there is the panel stage, that may take up to 45 days to be appointed, plus 6 months for its conclusion. The role of the panel is to help the DSB make rulings or recommendations based on the agreements cited. Since reports can only be rejected by consensus in the DSB, its conclusions may be difficult to overturn. The panel's final report should normally be given to the parties to the dispute within six months. In cases of urgency, including those concerning perishable goods, the deadline is shortened to three months.

Either side can appeal a panel's ruling based on points of law, but cannot reexamine existing evidence or examine new issues. Each appeal is heard by three members of a permanent seven-member Appellate Body set up by the DSB and broadly representing the range of WTO membership. The Appellate Body was established in 1995

[20] Gstohl and Schnock (2024, p. 58(1)).

[21] World Trade Organization (2024c).

[22] World Trade Organization (2024).

[23] Traditional forms of ADR, namely negotiation, mediation, conciliation, and arbitration, offer different approaches to resolving disagreements outside of the courtroom. Mediation involves a neutral third-party facilitating communication and negotiation between the disputing parties to help them reach a mutually agreeable solution. Conciliation is similar to mediation but often involves a more active role from the conciliator in suggesting potential solutions. Arbitration, on the other hand, is a more formal process where the parties present their cases to a neutral tribunal, which then makes a binding decision.

under Article 17 of the Understanding on Rules and Procedures Governing the Settlement of Disputes (DSU).[24] The Appellate Body can uphold, modify or reverse the legal findings and conclusions of a panel, and Appellate Body Reports are adopted by the DSB unless all members decide not to do so.

Currently, the Appellate Body is unable to review appeals due to its ongoing vacancies. The term of the last sitting Appellate Body member expired on 30 November 2020 and, as the United States has blocked new appointments since 2018, the body has been 'frozen' ever since.[25]

Despite the freezing of the WTO's Appellate Body, the DBS recently ruled over two cases that may pose implications to the EUDR. This could potentially mean the beginnings of what a precedent in terms of implementing rules with extraterritorial effects. The discussion relies mainly if EU norms with extraterritorial effects can be used as exceptions under the WTO, particularly in accordance with Article XX of the GATT.

In literature, some authors understand that forests constitute 'exhaustible natural resources' within the meaning of Article XX(g) GATT, considering the expansive and flexible interpretation of this term in WTO jurisprudence.[26] Yet, there are those who argue that not all extraterritorial measures falling under GATT's Article XX(g) should be accepted as legal, but only those imposed in good faith, with technical and financial assistance included, aimed at fighting common concerns of humankind in the form of conservation of some exhaustible natural resources.[27]

In general terms, the rules of the WTO allow for the use of trade-related environmental measures provided that they align with the principles of international trade law and are non-discriminatory in nature, thus preventing their abuse for protectionist purposes.[28] In this sense, one may inquire whether the EUDR falls under the exceptions[29] outlined in GATT's Article XX, specifically concerning its chapeau[30] and specifically the conditions established by provisions (b)[31] and (g).[32]

Article XX may correlate with process and production methods (PPMs). PPM refers to some countries' intention to regulate international trade in goods and services

---

[24] World Trade Organization (2024).

[25] Pelc (2024)

[26] Marín Durán and Scott (2022, p. 245).

[27] Vij (2023, p. 14).

[28] Dobson (2023).

[29] While WTO members have some leeway to implement trade policies that might conflict with GATT rules, they must justify these measures under specific exceptions within the WTO framework.

[30] GATT, Article XX: Subject to the requirement that such measures are not applied in a manner which would constitute a means of arbitrary or unjustifiable discrimination between countries where the same conditions prevail, or a disguised restriction on international trade, nothing in this Agreement shall be construed to prevent the adoption or enforcement by any contracting party of measures [...].

[31] GATT, Article XX(b): necessary to protect human, animal or plant life or health.

[32] GATT, Article XX(g): relating to the conservation of exhaustible natural resources if such measures are made effective in conjunction with restrictions on domestic production or consumption.

on the basis of the inputs and process technologies utilised in their production,[33] which is the case of the EUDR. Some WTO's cases discussed PPMs as their main contentious elements, particularly the US–Tuna Dolphin cases,[34] and US–Shrimp/Turtle[35] case.

Following the US–Tuna Dolphin cases,[36] the WTO's Appellate Body has devised an original approach for analysing article XX, called the 'two-tiered test'.[37] In this procedure, the WTO first checks: (i) whether the restrictive measures can be classified as exceptional situations, as they must be necessary to the protection of human, animal, and plant health; or relate to the conservation of exhaustible natural resources; and, then, (ii) analyses whether they are arbitrary or constitute unjustified discrimination.

This method was first developed in the United States-Reformulated Gasoline case,[38] followed by the US–Shrimp/Turtle case[39] and Brazil–Tyres,[40] further specifying how both exceptions must be interpreted. In the case of unilateral standard-setting, the Appellate Body in US–Shrimp-Turtle did not condemn them per se, potentially allowing exterritorial measures, but raised concerns on measures adopted without taking into consideration different conditions which may occur in the territories of those other Members.[41] Thus, the analytical framework to analyse Article XX has emerged as the standard practice for the organization.[42]

Also, WTO sought to establish additional methods for justifying environmental trade measures: (i) as measures undertaken for protection of public morals under GATT Article XX(a)[43]; and (ii) as non-tariff barriers under both Sanitary and phytosanitary measures (SPS) and TBT Agreements.[44]

Under this understanding, two recent cases involving have drawn attention by addressing the compatibility of EU norms with potential extraterritorial effects with the WTO framework. On 15 January 2021, the DS 600 Case[45] was established when Malaysia requested consultations with the EU, France and Lithuania with respect to certain measures imposed by the EU and EU Member States concerning palm oil and oil palm crop-based biofuels from Malaysia. Malaysia claimed that certain measures imposed by the EU appear to be inconsistent with the WTO framework, such as

---

33 Read (2005).

34 World Trade Organization (1994).

35 World Trade Organization (1996a).

36 World Trade Organization (1994).

37 Koul (2018).

38 World Trade Organization (1995).

39 World Trade Organization (1996).

40 World Trade Organization (2005).

41 World Trade Organization (1996).

42 M. Matsushita et al. (2015).

43 Matsushita et al. (2015).

44 The verification of arbitrariness of restrictive measures also applies in other WTO rules, such as the TBT and the SPS.

45 World Trade Organization (2024).

the EU renewable energy target, the criteria for determining the high ILUC-risk feedstock, and the sustainability and GHG emission savings criteria.

On 26 April 2024, the panel confirmed the overall compatibility of the EU regulations with the WTO, but noted that certain aspects of their application and design were incompatible with WTO rules, such as regarding its accordance with Article XX of the GATT. The panel found that the norm indeed falls under the case of conservation of exhaustible natural resources that was made effective in conjunction with restrictions on domestic consumption or production within the meaning of Article XX(g), as well as necessary to protect human, animal or plant life or health within the meaning of Article XX(b), and public morals under Article XX(a).

However, the panel found the norms had been administered in a manner that constituted arbitrary or unjustifiable discrimination between countries where the same conditions prevail, since the EU failed to conduct a timely review of the data used to determine which biofuels had high risk, and because there were deficiencies in the design and implementation of the low-risk criteria and certification procedure. In summary, the panel understanding was that the norm was compatible with the WTO framework, while certain aspects of the implementation and design were not. Therefore, even if the scope of the EU's norms complies with the WTO, their implementation cannot be conducted in an arbitrary or unjustifiably discriminatory manner.

Similarly, the DS 593, initiated by Indonesia in 2019, came to contest EU measures under RED II on palm oil and oil palm-based biofuels.[46] On 10 January 2025, WTO's panel upheld the EU's capacity to initiate environmental and climate-based measures in accordance with the Renewable Energy Directive (RED II), yet certain aspects of the implementation and design of an EU delegated act under the Directive were inconsistent with WTO rules.

In summary, the case started when Indonesia requested consultations with the EU pursuant to Article 4 of the DSU, Article XXII of the GATT, Article 14 of the TBT Agreement and Article 30 of the Agreement on Subsidies and Countervailing Measures (SCM Agreement) regarding the measures and claims concerning EU measures on palm oil and oil palm crop-based biofuels.

The WTO panel found that these measures were compatible with the TBT (and Indonesia failed to establish this incompatibility), but its requirements and phase-out were not due to deficiencies in the design and implementation of their criteria. With respect to Article XX of the GATT, the panel found that the measures relate to the conservation of exhaustible natural resources that is made effective in conjunction with restrictions on domestic production or consumption within the meaning of Article XX(g), as well as the necessity to protect human, animal or plant life or health within the meaning of Article XX(b). Despite that, Indonesia welcomed the ruling, as it expects to affect the EUDR concerning the legality of its implementation.[47]

---

[46] World Trade Organization (2025).

[47] Ziegler (2025).

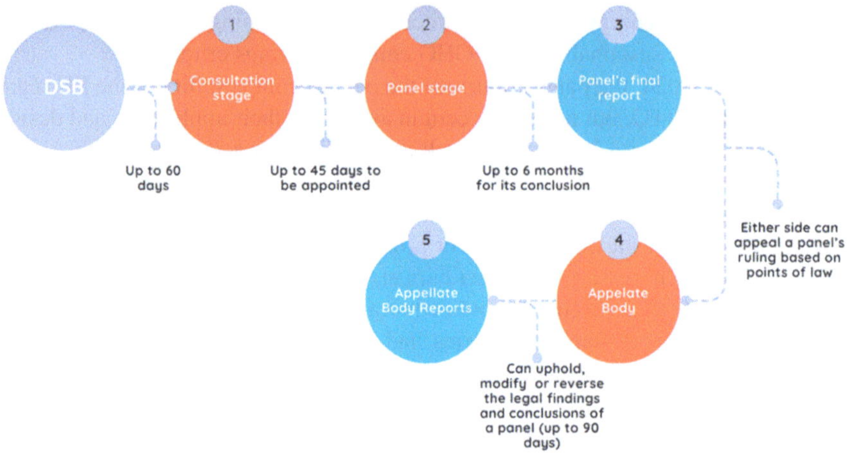

Fig. 4.2 DSB's flowchart

As observed, both cases recognised the compatibility of EU rules with the WTO framework, particularly Article XX. However, WTO's panels decided that the implementation of these rules was incompatible with the international trade regime. This can pose an initial line of understanding to future cases in the WTO. The visual representation of the DSB's flowchart is presented in Fig. 4.2.

4.1.3 The Committee on Trade and Environment

Due to the 'forced' Appellate Body paralysis, some alternatives have been pursued to circumvent the situation. One of them is the use of WTO's Committees as forum for dialogues. Particularly, the Committe on Trade and Environment (CTE) is used to treat trade-environmental-related themes, including EU norms such as the EUDR. The CTE was created on January 31,[48] 1995, following the Marrakesh Ministerial Decision on Trade and Environment (1994).[49] The CTE provided WTO members with a forum for debate, contributing to bridging the gap between trade and environmental concerns. With its broad mandate, the CTE has helped identify and understand the relationship between trade and environmental measures to promote sustainable development.[50]

As a space to discuss trade-environmental themes, the forum managed to encompass discussions on the EUDR. For instance, the 2022 CTE Annual Report to the

[48] World Trade Organization (2024).

[49] World Trade Organization (2004).

[50] World Trade Organization (2020).

Council for Trade in Goods[51] described how the issue was dealt with during the CTE meetings throughout the year.

At the February meeting, the EU briefed WTO delegations on the implementation of the European Green Deal, and particularly the EUDR. Several delegations recognized the importance of the objectives pursued by the European Green Deal and of the respect of the Common but Differentiated Responsibilities (CBDR) principle to avoid possible discriminations. Other delegations encouraged the EU to further consult with WTO Members in order to better develop the EUDR in compliance with the international trade regime. Broadly, the delegations noted that measures must consider economic, social, and environmental conditions and needs of developing countries; and comply with WTO rules.

Later at the June meeting, the EU continued briefing on trade aspects of the then upcoming EUDR under the framework of the Green Deal. At the October meeting, the EU updated on the status of certain proposals of importance to EU exporters. Several delegations took the opportunity to clarify the scope of the proposals and posed specific questions on the details of their implementation, in which the EU responded, stressing its transparency efforts, including in the CTE, and highlighting that the Green Deal measures do not intend to create barriers to trade, which also applied to the EUDR.

The 2023 Report further registered multilateral dialogues on the EUDR. At the March meeting, the European Union (EU) provided an update on the EUDR and other norms. Then on the November meeting, Paraguay on behalf of Argentina, Brazil, Colombia, Ecuador, Guatemala, Honduras, Mexico and Peru introduced a new communication on the EUDR expressing 'concern about this unilateral standard that imposes a trade measure that could generate higher costs or barriers to trade, especially for small businesses and producers in chains of great importance to our countries'.[52] The 2024 CTE Annual Report[53] brought the most recent debate on the EUDR throughout the year. EU main statements revolved around its workings on guidelines to clarify and address technical issues, including to use of certification scheme to facilitate compliance with due diligence requirements, and definition of agriculture use, as well as the benchmarking of country-risk methodology.[54] Other countries enquired about uncertainties on the benchmarking system, data that needs to be supplied as part of the due diligence process, possible impact on smallholders in producing countries as well as its potential inconsistencies with WTO rules. Also, some Members requested impact assessment, further consultations or a delay in the implementation.[55]

Thus, the CTE has been used as a forum of discussion for trade-environmental themes, including EU regulations such as the EUDR. Potentially, the CTE may foster

---

[51] World Trade Organization. WT/CTE/29 (2022c).

[52] World Trade Organization. WT/CTE/GEN/33 (2023c).

[53] World Trade Organization. WT/CTE/31 (2024f).

[54] See Article 29 of the EUDR. All countries shall be initially classified as 'standard risk'. In the case of Brazil, this was further confirmed by the EU.

[55] Summing up to the international pressure for a postponement.

Fig. 4.3 MPIA's overview

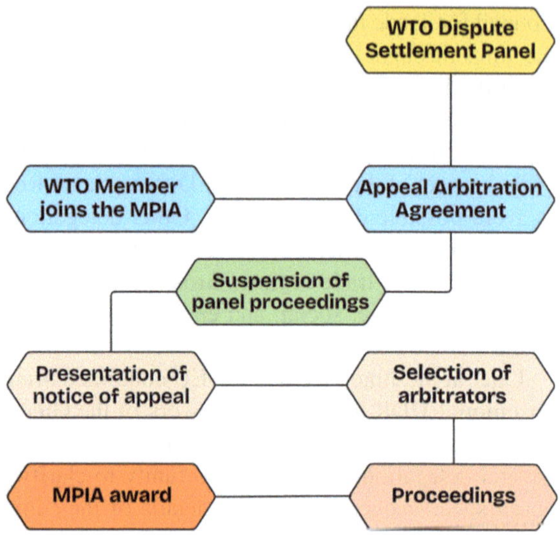

friendly dialogues to settle doubts and resolve possible disputes when it comes to implementing the EUDR without the need to resort to the DSB.

4.1.4 The MPIA

Other alternative encompasses fostering alternative dispute resolution mechanism within the WTO framework. In this sense, the Multi-Party Interim Appeal Arbitration Arrangement (MPIA) has gained prominence as an institution of arbitration aimed at resolving trade-related disputes during the WTO paralysis.

Alongside the potential use of the CTE, the MPIA came in 2020 as a specific alternative to the paralysis of the WTO.[56] WTO members can resort to the use of the MPIA under Article 25 of the WTO Dispute Settlement Understanding (DSU), as an alternative mechanism for dispute settlement. In 2025, the MPIA had nearly 30 members, including Brazil and EU; and 3 ongoing disputes, 2 finalized cases and 8 withdrawn, lapsed or settled disputes.[57] Figure 4.3 presents an overview of the MPIA.

Procedures under the MPIA follow a certain structure.[58] Firstly, a WTO Member decides to join the MPIA. Upon establishment of a WTO Dispute Settlement Panel, the parties conclude an appeal arbitration agreement. Then, if a party wants to appeal, it can request the suspension of panel proceedings before the panel report is circulated. For the initiation of the MPIA, either party shall present a notice of appeal. The MPIA

[56] WTO Plurilaterals (2025).

[57] Ibid.

[58] Pauwelyn (2023).

consists of a pool of 10 arbitrators, selected by consensus of all MPIA participants in July 2020. A panel of three is randomly selected from among the arbitrator pool of ten. Appellee (or response) have 18 days to fill in submissions. By day 21, third parties in the dispute (which may or may not be MPIA participants) can file a third-party submission. Between day 30 and day 45, oral hearings take place. By day 90 at the latest, the MPIA arbitrators must issue their award to the parties. Finally, the MPIA award is issued in WTO's three official languages and includes the panel's un-appealed findings and any decisions made by the arbitrators.

As mentioned, the MPIA has contributed to the conclusion of two cases involving trade-related disputes. The first case was the DS583 'EU v. Turkey — Certain Measures concerning the Production, Importation and Marketing of Pharmaceutical Products'.[59] Although Turkey was not a MPIA member, the disputing parties did enter into an appeal-arbitration agreement under DSU Article 25 that respects the principles of the MPIA, and two of the three arbitrators that heard this appeal arbitration were drawn from the MPIA pool of arbitrators.

The case initiated in 2019 when the EU requested consultations with Turkey regarding several measures concerning the production, importation and marketing of pharmaceutical products and their incompatibility with WTO rules. These measures included localisation requirement, technology transfer requirement, import ban on localised products, and prioritization measure. After its full analysis, the panel recognised the EU's claims. Then, the parties agreed to set procedures for arbitration under Article 25 of the DSU, in which the panel's findings were upheld by arbitrators. On 18 August 2022, due to the decision, Türkiye informed the DSB that it intended to implement the recommendations and rulings of the arbitrators and the panel in this dispute in a manner that respects its WTO obligations and that it would need a reasonable period of time to do so, which was set, under mutual consensus of the parties, to expire on 25 April 2023.

The second case, DS591 'EU v. Colombia — Anti-Dumping Duties on Frozen Fries from Belgium, Germany and the Netherlands',[60] was decided by MPIA arbitrators on 21 December 2022. The case started on 15 November 2019, when the EU requested consultations with Colombia regarding the anti-dumping duties imposed by Colombia on imports of potatoes. Later on 17 February 2020, the EU requested the establishment of a panel. On 13 July 2020, both parties informed the DSB that they had agreed to Procedures for Arbitration under Article 25 of the DSU in the dispute. These procedures, which were subsequently revised on 20 April 2021, were entered into by the parties to give effect to MPIA and to decide any appeal from any final panel report as issued to the parties in the dispute. Following the agreement of the parties, the panel was composed on 24 August 2020. Later, by October 2022, arbitrators found that Colombia acted inconsistently with the WTO framework. Considering the findings, on 10 March 2023, the parties informed the DSB they had agreed on a reasonable period of time for Colombia to implement the recommendations of the arbitrators, which would expire on 5 November 2023.

[59] World Trade Organization (2019b).

[60] World Trade Organization (2019a).

As observed, both cases were in development after the beginning of the WTO Appeal Body 'freeze' and resorted to arbitration as an alternative mechanism to dispute settlement. After the procedures were carried out, the parties agreed on the implementation of the recommended findings. In this sense, the two cases can be seen as successful in terms of dispute settlement recognised by parties, including the EU, and in line with the WTO framework.

4.2 Alternative Dispute Resolution Mechanisms in Bilateral Agreements

4.2.1 Free Trade Agreements

Recent bilateral treaties between the EU and its partners, such as Chile and Singapore, dedicate an entire section within its dispute settlement chapter to a detailed mediation procedure. This specific provision outlines the steps involved in bilateral mediation, including procedures for requesting mediation, selecting mediators, conducting the mediation process, and addressing the outcomes. Such explicit inclusion of mediation within the agreement demonstrates a commitment to utilizing diplomatic and political ADR methods as a primary means of resolving disagreements related to the interpretation or application of the agreement's provisions. This proactive approach can be more efficient and less adversarial than resorting to formal dispute settlement through a panel or tribunal, allowing the parties to maintain their trading relationship while addressing their concerns.

While the WTO's DSU allows for mediation (Article 5), it's rarely used due to a lack of clear procedural rules regarding mediator selection, process, outcome relevance, and its relationship with arbitration. The EU's bilateral FTAs address these shortcomings to encourage greater use of mediation.

The EU includes mediation mechanisms in its FTAs because it offers a faster and cheaper way to resolve trade issues. FTA dispute settlement can take around six months, whereas mediation is designed to last only two.

Mediation is voluntary, requiring both parties' consent. If they can't agree on a mediator, one is chosen from the roster of arbitration panel chairpersons. The process is flexible, focusing on the mediator proposing a solution. Agreed solutions are binding and must be implemented. To protect the mediation process, any evidence used cannot be introduced in subsequent formal dispute settlement proceedings under the FTA or any other agreement.

The EU-Singapore Free Trade Agreement FTA goes beyond traditional dispute settlement mechanisms by incorporating specific non-judicial processes within its TSD chapter. These mechanisms acknowledge the unique nature of TSD issues and aim to resolve disagreements through cooperative and less adversarial approaches.

One such mechanism is Government Consultations. This process allows the parties to engage in direct discussions to address concerns or disagreements related to the implementation or interpretation of the TSD provisions. It provides a platform for open communication and information sharing, enabling the parties to better understand each other's perspectives and potentially find mutually acceptable solutions.

In addition to consultations, the EU-Singapore FTA provides for a Panel of Experts. This mechanism involves the establishment of an independent panel composed of experts in relevant fields, who are tasked with reviewing specific TSD-related issues and providing recommendations to the parties. The Panel of Experts serves as an objective and impartial body, offering expert analysis and guidance on complex matters.

Beyond these specific mechanisms, the TSD chapter also includes general provisions on cooperation between the parties. These provisions underscore the commitment to ongoing dialogue and collaboration on TSD matters, including: assessing the FTA's environmental impact; collaborating in international environmental fora (WTO, UNEP, MEAs); promoting MEA ratification and implementation; cooperating on certification and labeling schemes, including green public procurement; discussing the trade impact of environmental regulations; cooperating on climate change-related trade issues; collaborating on MEA-related trade aspects; cooperating on sustainable forest management; discussing the relationship between MEAs and trade rules; discussing environmental goods and services liberalization; and exchanging views on marine resource management.

The EU-Mercosur Association Agreement, concluded in December 2024, lays out a general structured approach to dispute settlement, beginning with mechanisms aimed at amicable resolution before resorting to formal arbitration. Section B of the dispute settlement chapter explicitly details the processes of consultations and mediation within this general framework, although specific mechanisms exist for trade and sustainability disputes elsewhere in the agreement. Article XX.5 mandates that the parties first endeavour to resolve any disputes concerning alleged non-compliance with the covered provisions of Part X or allegations of nullification or substantial impairment of benefits through good faith consultations. This initial phase underscores the importance of diplomatic engagement and seeks to achieve a mutually agreed solution, even acknowledging the specific challenges faced by landlocked developing countries within this context. The process is initiated by a written request outlining the issue, the measures in question, and the specific provisions or benefits affected. Strict timelines are established for holding and concluding consultations, emphasizing the need for a swift response, particularly in urgent matters involving perishable goods. The confidentiality of these consultations and the positions taken are also ensured, preserving the rights of the parties in any subsequent proceedings should a resolution not be reached.

Should consultations fail to yield a mutually agreed solution within the stipulated timeframes, or if a party believes that the other has not complied with a solution agreed upon during consultations, the agreement provides recourse to further amicable means through mediation, as outlined in Article XX.6 and Annex XX.C. Mediation, however, differs from consultations in that it can only be initiated by mutual consensus of the parties involved. This voluntary nature highlights the reliance on the willingness of both sides to engage in a facilitated process aimed at finding a resolution that may go beyond the strict legal interpretations of the agreement. While the agreement does not detail the specifics of the mediation process within the main text, the reference to Annex XX.C suggests a more elaborated framework for how mediation would be conducted, potentially involving a neutral third party to assist the parties in reaching a mutually acceptable outcome. The inclusion of both consultations and mediation underscores a preference for resolving disputes through cooperative dialogue and negotiated settlements before moving to the more adversarial process of arbitration.

4.2.2 TSD Chapter

From 2011 onwards, trade agreements with the EU have included a chapter on TSD.[61] These agreements incorporate three main elements that are present in the majority of TSD chapters.[62] Firstly, there are commitments by the parties.[63] Secondly, the chapter includes structures that facilitate the involvement of civil society in the monitoring of the implementation of these commitments.[64] Thirdly, a specific dispute resolution mechanism is set to address potential breaches of these commitments. The precise contents, structure and functioning of each TSD Chapter vary from agreement to agreement.

In this respect, the content of the EU-Mercosur Agreement TSD chapter appears to be consistent with a dominant model of EU trade agreements negotiated by the EU Commission. The EU-Mercosur agreement exhibits similarities with other trade agreements. A substantial degree of similarity is found in the structure and content of many of the partnership agreements concluded by the EU Commission. These agreements may also have intersections with the scope of the EUDR. Any controversy involving a TSD matter may be addressed through the dispute settlement mechanisms established in these agreements. In order to conduct this analysis, the EU-Mercosur agreement will be compared to the EU-Canada Comprehensive Economic and Trade Agreement (CETA), the EU-Chile Interim Trade Agreement (ITA) and the EU-Singapore Free-Trade Agreement (EUSFTA).

Particularly, the EU-Mercosur Partnership Agreement[65] provides a forum for discussion of 'Trade and Sustainable Development' (TSD). The agreement's TSD

[61] Fern (2020, p. 2).

[62] Ibid., p. 2.

[63] Ibid., p. 2.

[64] Ibid., p. 2.

[65] European Union, 'EU-Mercosur: Text of the Agreement'. https://policy.trade.ec.europa.eu/eu-trade-relationships-country-and-region/countries-and-regions/mercosur/eu-mercosuragreement/text-agreement_en. Accessed 13 January 2025.

Chapter sets out commitments pertaining to sustainable development, with the objective of fostering a collaborative enhancement in the integration of sustainable development into the trade and investment relationship between the EU and Mercosur. This chapter may offer several points of contact with the EUDR, particularly concerning international environmental agreements compliance,[66] and measures to protect forests[67] and mitigate climate change.[68] The Agreement also provides for the establishment within a year of its entry into force a list of products from Mercosur countries which may contribute to the conservation, restoration, sustainable use and management of forests and vulnerable ecosystems. Products in this list, which shall be periodically reviewed every three years, should be granted preferential/additional market access, or other incentives by the EU to promote their trade, such as technical assistance, capacity building. Although no product has been formally indicated as part of this list, this may potentially include products covered by the EUDR, serving as a mean to facilitate and regulate operations regarding these specific goods under the EU norm requirements.

Lastly, the TSD Chapter establish a specific dispute resolution chapter, providing for a more 'attenuated' mechanism involving monitoring and consultation by a joint TSD subcommittee and a panel of experts. This means that, instead of being subject to the general dispute settlement mechanism under the Agreement,[69] disputes relating to TSD matters will be governed by the provisions of the TSD chapter of the agreement. Relevant contribution is Article 14 of the Chapter, which establishes a Sub-Committee on Trade and Sustainable Development (TSD Sub-Committee). The TSD Sub-Committee will be responsible for facilitating and monitoring the effective implementation of the Chapter, including cooperation activities undertaken under its scope, carrying out consultation and making recommendations. This Sub-Committee may serve as a focal point for addressing issues of trade and sustainability, such as those related to the scope of the EUDR.

A significant critique of the TSD chapter concerns the weakness of its enforcement system. In contrast to the general dispute resolution chapter, the TSD chapter is dependent solely on the so-called Domestic Advisory Groups (DGA's), consisting of independent representatives from civil society organisations.[70] These groups are only empowered to undertake monitoring of the implementation of the chapter, and as a result, no trade sanctions system is in place to address disputes involving TSD.[71]

---

[66] See Article 5 of the TSD Chapter.

[67] See Article 7 and 8 of the TSD Chapter.

[68] See Article 6 of the TSD Chapter.

[69] The Dispute Resolution Chapter establishes a comprehensive mechanism for resolving disputes between the parties, covering both issues of interpretation and application of the Agreement and the preservation of the balance of concessions, even in the absence of explicit violations of the terms. The process begins with consultations between the parties, seeking an amicable solution. If the consultations do not result in an agreement, mediation can be used, provided there is mutual consensus. If these steps are unsuccessful, one of the parties can request the formation of an arbitration panel to assess the compliance of specific measures with the obligations set out in the Agreement.

[70] Fern (2020 (n1), p. 5).

[71] Ibid., p. 5.

With regard to TSD disputes, these bilateral agreements contain two main dispute resolution mechanisms: a Consultation Procedure and a Panel of Experts. When a dispute arises, the Parties are required to initiate a consultation with the other party involved. This mechanism consists of the delivery of a request by one party to the other, with the intention of finding a solution to a dispute. Within the consultations mechanism, a specialised TSD body may be convened to address the issue when the parties consider further discussion to be necessary. Subsequently, in the event that no mutually satisfactory solution has been reached within the stipulated timeframe, the Parties may request the establishment of a Panel of Experts. This mechanism refers to the analysis of the matter by a number of experts, as indicated by the Parties involved, in accordance with the norms of each agreement.

The dispute resolution mechanisms in the bilateral agreements are categorised in Table 4.3.

4.2.2.1 Consultation Procedure

The EU-Mercosur Agreement establishes a consultation procedure in Article 16 of the TSD Chapter. A Party may request consultations with the other Party on the interpretation or application of this chapter by delivering a written request to the contact point of the other Party. The Parties shall enter into consultations with a view to reaching a mutually satisfactory resolution of the matter. This procedure shall commence promptly after a Party delivers a request for consultations, and in any event not later than 30 days from the date of receipt of the request. Consultations shall begin promptly after a Party delivers a request for consultations, and in any case not later than 30 days after the date of receipt of the request. If they are to be held in person, the meetings shall be held on the territory of the Party receiving the request, unless otherwise agreed by the Parties. Article 16 of the EU-Mercosur Agreement stipulates that the TSD Sub-Committee shall be convened whenever a Party considers that the matter requires further discussion. Such a request shall be made no earlier than 60 days from the date of receipt of the request. The TSD Sub-Committee shall meet as soon as possible and shall endeavour to reach a mutually satisfactory resolution of the matter. It also provides that any resolution reached by the Parties shall be made available to the public. Each Party or the Sub-Committee on TSD may seek the views of the DGA's.

CETA provides for the consultation procedure in Article 24.14 of the Trade and Environment Chapter. This chapter is the equivalent of the other agreements TSD chapter. Similarly, a Party to CETA may request consultations with the other Party on any matter arising under this Chapter by submitting a written request to the other Party's designated point of contact. The Party shall present the matter clearly in the request, identify the issues at stake, and provide a brief summary of any claim under this Chapter. The procedure shall commence promptly after the delivery by the Party of a request for consultations. CETA establishes a Committee on TSD. It is stipulated in Article 22.4, and it shall be convened when a party to the CETA considers that

Table 4.3 Comparison between the TSD dispute resolution mechanisms in bilateral agreements

TSD dispute resolution mechanisms				
	EU-Mercosur	CETA	ITA	EUSFTA
Consultations	Article 16, (1) (TSD Chapter)—Consultations	Article 24.14, (1). (Trade and Environment Chapter)—Consultations	Article 26.21, (1). (TSD Chapter)—Consultations	Article 12.16, (2). (TSD Chapter)—Government Consultations
Panel of Experts	Article 17, (1). (TSD Chapter)—Panel of experts	Article 24.15, (1). (Trade and Environment Chapter)—Panel of experts	Article 26.22, (1). (TSD Chapter)—Panel of Experts	Article 12.17, (1). (TSD Chapter)—Panel of Experts

further discussion is necessary. CETA provides for the establishment of domestic advisory groups, to seek views and advice on issues relating to this chapter.

Article 26.21 of the ITA Chapter on TSD provides for this procedure. The Agreement stipulates that a Party may, at any time, request consultations with the other Party on any matter relating to the interpretation or application of this chapter by submitting a written request to the contact point of the responding Party. This agreement also specifies that the Parties shall enter into consultations with a view to resolving the matter in a mutually satisfactory manner. The request shall indicate the reasons for requesting consultations, including a sufficiently specific description of the matter in question and its relation to the provisions of this chapter. Unless otherwise agreed, the Parties shall commence consultations no later than 30 days after the date of receipt of the request by the responding Party. The procedure may be held in person or by any technological means available to the Parties.

ITA also stipulates that, in the event of consultations in person, these shall take place on the territory of the responding Party, unless otherwise mutually agreed by the Parties. Article 26.21 of the ITA establishes a Sub-Committee on TSD. This body may be convened at the request of either Party if the parties are unable to resolve the matter within 60 days of the request for consultations. In line with other agreements, it provides that it shall be convened in a timely manner to agree on a resolution of the matter. The agreement stipulates that the Sub-Committee on TSD or the Parties may solicit the perspectives of domestic civil society bodies established within the framework of the agreement.

In the EUSFTA, the consultation procedure is established in Article 12.16. In case of disagreement on any matter arising under this chapter, the Agreement underscores that the Parties are only permitted to resort to the procedures stipulated in the TSD Chapter. A Party to EUSFTA may request consultations by delivering a written request to the contact point of the other Party. Consultations shall commence at the earliest opportunity following a Party's submission of a request for consultations. The agreement also provides that the Parties shall make every effort to reach a mutually satisfactory resolution of the matter. Employing a distinct nomenclature, the EUFTA establishes a Board on TSD, rather than a Committee or a Sub-Committee. As delineated in Article 12.15, the composition of the Board is to be comprised of senior officials from the respective administrations of the Parties. The Board shall convene within the initial two years following the date of entry into force of the Agreement. Subsequent meetings are to be scheduled as and when required, with the objective of ensuring the effective implementation of the TSD Chapter. EUSFTA also establishes domestic advisory groups, which may submit views to the parties on the implementation of the chapter.

4.2.2.2 Panel of Experts

In the EU-Mercosur agreement, Article 17 of the TSD chapter provides for the establishment of a Panel of Experts. If, within 120 days of a request for consultations under Article 16, no mutually satisfactory resolution has been reached, a Party may request the establishment of a Panel of Experts to examine the matter. The request for the establishment of a Panel of Experts shall be submitted in written form to the designated contact point of the other party. This request is to include a detailed justification outlining the rationale for the establishment of the aforementioned Panel of Experts. The terms of reference for the Panel of Experts will be to examine the matter referred to in the request for its establishment in the light of the relevant provisions of Chapter 17 of the EU-Mercosur Association Agreement, and to issue a report, making recommendations for the resolution of the matter.

The Panel of Experts will interpret the provisions of the TSD Chapter in accordance with the customary rules of interpretation of public international law. The Panel is required to issue an interim report to the Parties within 90 days of the Panel's establishment, and a final report no later than 60 days after the issuance of the interim report. These reports shall meticulously delineate the findings, the applicability of the relevant provisions, and the fundamental rationale underpinning the findings and recommendations. In addition, the Agreement establishes Domestic Advisory Groups, which, as outlined in Article 17, are empowered to monitor the follow-up to the report of the Panel of Experts and its recommendations.

CETA establishes a Panel of Experts mechanism in Article 24.15 of the Trade and Environment Chapter. This provision stipulates that a Panel of Experts shall be convened for any matter that is not satisfactorily addressed through consultations. A Party may request the formation of a Panel of Experts to examine a given matter by delivering a written request to the designated contact point of the other Party, no later than 90 days after the receipt of the initial request for consultations. The Panel of Experts is to be constituted of three panellists. The Parties shall undertake consultations with a view to reaching an agreement on the composition of the Panel of Experts within 10 working days of the receipt by the responding Party of a request for the establishment of a Panel of Experts. The experts to be proposed as panellists must have specialised knowledge or expertise in environmental law, issues addressed in the Chapter, or in the resolution of disputes arising under international agreements. They are required to be independent in their actions and decision-making, and not take instructions from any organisation or government with regard to the matter in issue.

The Panel shall issue an interim report and a final report to the Parties, setting out the findings of fact, its determinations on the matter, including as to whether the responding Party has conformed with its obligations under this chapter, and the rationale behind any findings. The terms of reference for the establishment of the Panel of Experts will be to examine the matter referred to in the request for the establishment of the Panel in the light of the relevant provisions of the Trade and Environment Chapter, and to deliver a report that makes recommendations for resolving the matter.

ITA provides for the Panel of Experts in Article 26.22 of the TSD Chapter. This provision stipulates that a Party may request the establishment of a Panel to examine the matter if no mutually satisfactory resolution has been reached within 60 days of the delivery of a written request for consideration of a matter by the Sub-Committee on TSD, or if no such request is made, within 120 days of the delivery of a written request for consultations. The request for the establishment of a Panel of Experts must include a detailed justification, including a comprehensive description of the matter at hand and a clear articulation of how this matter constitutes a breach of the covered provision(s) of the chapter in question. The terms of reference of the Panel are as follows: to examine, in the light of the relevant provisions of the TSD Chapter of the EU-Chile Association Agreement, the matter referred to in the request for the establishment of the Panel of Experts, and to issue a report with its findings and recommendations for the resolution of the matter.

In a similar context, the Panel of Experts is required to interpret the provisions of this chapter in accordance with the customary rules of interpretation of public international law, including those codified in the 1969 Vienna Convention on the Law of Treaties. The panel is required to submit an interim report and a final report, which will present the findings of fact, the applicability of the relevant provisions, and the rationale behind these findings. In the event that the Panel of Experts determines that a Party has not fulfilled its obligations under this chapter, the Parties shall enter into discussions concerning the implementation of appropriate measures, taking into account the report and recommendations of the Panel.

EUSFTA incorporates a Panel of Experts procedure in Article 12.17. This mechanism is triggered when the Board has not addressed a matter satisfactorily within 120 days of receiving a request to convene to consider that matter, or within a longer period as agreed by both Parties. In such an event, a Party may request, by delivering a written request to the contact point of the other Party, that a Panel of Experts be established to examine that matter. The members of the Panel shall be individuals with specialised knowledge or expertise regarding the issues addressed in the Chapter, regarding labour or environmental law, or regarding the resolution of disputes arising under international agreements. This provision also establishes the requirement that the individuals concerned shall be independent and not permitted to take instructions from any organisation or government with regard to issues related to the matter at stake. They are prohibited from having any affiliation with the government of Singapore, the government of any Member State of the EU, or the EU itself. The terms of reference of the Panel shall be as follows: The Panel will examine the matter referred to in the request for the establishment of the Panel of Experts, in light of the relevant provisions of the TSD Chapter. The Panel shall also issue an interim report and a final report, presenting the findings of fact, the applicability of the relevant provisions, and the fundamental rationale behind any findings and recommendations.

In summary, these bilateral agreements have in common a specific chapter for the resolution of disputes on TSD matters. The initial step is the consultation procedure, which is outlined in Articles 16, (1) of the EU-Mercosur, 24.14, (1) of the CETA, 26.21, (1) of the ITA and 12.16, (2) of the EUSFTA. After consultations, in the absence of a mutually agreed solution, the agreements stipulate the constitution of a panel of experts. This mechanism is set out in Article 17 (1) of the EU-Mercosur, Article 25.15 of the CETA, Article 26.22 (1) of the ITA and Article 12.17 (1) of the EUSFTA.

4.3 Grievance Mechanisms

Corporate grievance mechanisms are internal processes established by companies to allow stakeholders to raise concerns about the company's operations, particularly regarding environmental or human rights impacts. These mechanisms are designed to provide timely and effective resolutions within the company's operational framework. However, unlike the provisions in the EUDR, corporate grievance mechanisms are company-led and may lack the enforcement power of state authorities. The main goal is to resolve a grievance within the corporate governance and avoid further judicial processes. These mechanisms provide for continuous monitoring as they allow affected parties and stakeholders to file a complaint whenever a risk is identified.

Although the EUDR does not envisage grievance mechanisms, it incorporates provisions that allow external parties to raise concerns about non-compliance. For instance, Articles 31 and 32 provide mechanisms that enable stakeholders to report potential violations and seek legal remedies.

Article 31 introduces the concept of substantiated concerns,[72] allowing any natural or legal person to submit information to competent authorities if they believe an operator or trader is violating the regulation. Upon receiving such concerns, authorities are required to assess the information and, if necessary, take appropriate action, such as conducting investigations or implementing enforcement measures.

Moreover, Article 32 guarantees access to justice for individuals or entities with a sufficient interest, enabling them to challenge decisions, acts, or omissions of competent authorities regarding the enforcement of the regulation.[73] If an authority fails to act on a substantiated concern or makes a questionable decision, affected parties can seek judicial review or other legal remedies.

As the EUDR is inserted in a broader regulatory context under the Green Deal framework, complementarity with other norms could potentially be explored. Particularly, this is the case with the Corporate Sustainability Due Diligence Directive (CSDDD).[74] According to Article 1 (3) of the CSDDD, if a provision of the norm conflicts with a provision of another act pursuing the same objectives and providing for more extensive or more specific obligations, the provision of that other legislative act shall prevail to the extent of the conflict and shall apply as regards those specific obligations. Thus, while the CSDDD serves a broader regulation for sustainable value chains regulation (*lex generalis*), the EUDR brings specific dispositions on forest-related supply chains (*lex specialis*).

Therefore, the CSDDD provides a clear framework for the establishment of mechanisms for corporate responsibility and could potentially be regarded as a means of addressing the complaint mechanism gap within the EUDR framework. Under the CSDDD, companies are required to set up complaint mechanisms that enable stakeholders, including individuals and affected communities, to submit complaints

---

[72] See Article 31 of the EUDR.

[73] See Article 32 of the EUDR.

[74] European Council (2023).

regarding corporate practices. These mechanisms serve as a tool for holding companies accountable and ensuring compliance with sustainability standards in the EU.[75]

The CSDDD also mandates that companies implement processes enabling individuals and entities to submit complaints regarding actual or potential adverse impacts related to the companies' operations, their subsidiaries, or their business partners.[76] It outlines the categories of eligible complainants, the requirements for the complaint's procedure, and measures to protect complainants from retaliation.[77]

The CSDDD states that companies must set up a fair, transparent, and accessible process for handling complaints and ensure relevant workers and their representatives are informed. Additionally, they should provide a mechanism for individuals and organisations to report concerns about potential adverse impacts. To ease the burden, companies may join collective complaint mechanisms, such as those run by industry groups or multi-stakeholder initiatives. These mechanisms must align with international standards, ensuring they are legitimate, accessible, and rights-compatible, without undermining trade unions or collective bargaining rights. Companies should also address barriers that may prevent stakeholders from using these mechanisms effectively.[78] The scope of these processes is left to the discretion of companies, provided they comply with the mentioned criteria set by the CSDDD.

The Frequently Asked Questions (FAQ) document[79] published by the European Commission on the CSDDD highlights the Directive's capacity to enhance individuals' ability to hold companies accountable. This includes expanded rights to file complaints directly with companies, supervisory authorities, or courts. Additionally, it improves access to remedies for victims of human rights or environmental harms by providing both judicial avenues, such as civil liability claims, and non-judicial mechanisms, including company-established grievance processes.

In particular, grievance mechanisms such as those similar to CSDDD's provisions may serve as a tool for low-risk dispute settlement, as they function both as a preventive measure and as an alternative to judicial proceedings. When effectively implemented, they provide companies with structured channels—such as hotlines, complaint procedures, and conciliation mechanisms—through which stakeholders can raise concerns before they escalate into full-fledged disputes. By allowing companies to identify and address grievances at an early stage, these mechanisms contribute to dispute avoidance, thereby reducing the likelihood of costly and time-consuming dispute. In this sense, they act as a de-escalation tool, ensuring that grievances are handled internally and efficiently rather than turning into legal conflicts.

Furthermore, grievance mechanisms align with the principles of alternatives dispute resolution mechanisms by offering non-judicial solutions that facilitate dialogue and negotiated settlements. Processes such as mediation and conciliation,

---

[75] EUR-Lex (2024).

[76] See Article 14 of the CSDDD.

[77] Ibid.

[78] See para. 559 of the CSDDD.

[79] European Commission (2024a).

which may be embedded within grievance mechanisms, allow affected individuals and businesses to reach amicable agreements that prioritise problem-solving over adversarial dispute. This approach benefits both companies and individuals as companies can avoid judicial proceedings that might damage their reputation, work on strategies right their wrongs while affected individuals gain access to timely and cost-effective remedies. The flexibility of grievance mechanisms ensures that disputes are resolved in ways that are proportionate to the nature of the complaint, minimising legal risks and enhancing trust in corporate due diligence processes.

Additionally, by integrating grievance mechanisms into their corporate governance frameworks, companies demonstrate proactive compliance with regulatory requirements, including those under the CSDDD. This proactive approach not only mitigates the risk of formal disputes but also strengthens corporate accountability and transparency. Given that many sustainability-related disputes arise from gaps in communication or the absence of accessible reporting channels, grievance mechanisms function as a safeguard, ensuring that grievances do not escalate into judicial claims. When designed in line with international best practices, these mechanisms can offer robust procedural guarantees that instil confidence among stakeholders, reinforcing their effectiveness as a low-risk method of dispute resolution.

The discussion, however, may be impacted by a potential EU's regulatory shift. In November 2024, the President of the EU Commission Ursula von der Leyen announced the EU's new Omnibus Regulation, which aims to simplify the obligations under the CSDDD and other environmental norms, such as the Corporate Sustainability Reporting Directive (CSRD)[80] and the EU Taxonomy Regulation.[81] This initiative has been met with some criticism. For instance, some EU's legislative representatives argued that the lack of impact assessment and open consultation can be a smokescreen for deregulation.[82] However, the EUDR was not included (at least in the first package) among those norms to be 'simplified'. But, as companies may mix EUDR's due diligence procedures with those from other norms, there may be some impacts concerning government policies which encompass EUDR requirements.

4.4 Private International Law Mechanisms

Beyond the WTO framework and potential trade agreements, a comprehensive understanding of private international law (PIL) may contribute to EUDR-related issues and trade dynamics.

The production and distribution networks involved in the supply chains of goods covered by the EUDR are typically governed by a complex web of international commercial contracts. These contracts dictate the terms of trade between

80 EUR-Lex (2022).

81 EUR-Lex (2020).

82 Canfin (2025).

various actors, including small-scale producers, intermediaries (such as traders), and ultimately, the European Union market.

Private international law applicable to international commercial contracts furnishes a conceptual framework for envisioning potential scenarios of conflict arising from contractual disputes between entities of distinct national origins. Disputes arising from sustainability-related issues, such as those stemming from regulations like the EUDR, introduce novel complexities. These disputes may involve allegations of contract breaches arising from:

- Non-compliance with environmental regulations: For instance, a dispute may arise where a supplier fails to demonstrate compliance with the EUDR, leading to the rejection of goods by the buyer and subsequent contractual disputes regarding damages or termination.
- Unforeseen regulatory changes: As exemplified by the EUDR, evolving sustainability regulations can significantly impact contractual obligations. Disputes may arise when unforeseen regulatory shifts render contractual performance impossible or excessively burdensome, leading to claims of *force majeure* or frustration of contract.
- Disagreements over the interpretation of sustainability clauses: Many modern contracts now include provisions related to sustainability, such as commitments to environmental standards like the EUDR. Disputes may arise concerning the interpretation and enforcement of these clauses, particularly when their application is ambiguous or contested.

Some examples concerning the Brazilian case, which will be further analysed in the next chapter, can be found below.

4.4.1 *Jurisdiction*

The complexity of international supply chains can lead to disputes involving parties from diverse legal systems and transactions that cross multiple national boundaries. Private international law provides a framework for resolving jurisdictional conflicts in international commercial disputes by establishing rules for determining which jurisdiction can entertain such cases.

Moreover, it offers rules for interpreting contractual provisions that allow parties to choose between arbitration or judicial disputes before national courts, respecting their autonomy in selecting the dispute resolution method.

In the Brazilian domestic legal system, the exercise of jurisdiction by the Brazilian Judiciary is mainly regulated by articles 21 to 25 of the 2015 Brazilian Code of Civil Procedure (Federal Law n.° 13.105/2015).[83] Supplementary rules are provided by

[83] Brazil (2015).

the Introductory Law to the Norms of Brazilian Law (Law-Decree n.º 4.657/1942, LINDB).[84]

Article 21 outlines instances of concurrent jurisdiction for Brazil, meaning situations where Brazilian courts have jurisdiction alongside another country. These instances include: (i) when the defendant resides in Brazil; (ii) when the contractual obligation is to be fulfilled within Brazil; and (iii) when the cause of action arises from an event occurring or an act performed within Brazilian territory. Notably, the sole paragraph of this article stipulates that a foreign company with an agency or branch in Brazil is considered to be domiciled within the country.

4.4.2 Choice-of-Forum Clauses

Under Article 25, choice-of-forum clauses establishing the exclusive competence of a foreign court to judge a case will be valid and will prevent Brazilian courts from hearing such disputes, as long as they do not fall under the hypothesis of exclusive jurisdiction indicated in Article 23. Article 63(1) Code of Civil Procedure requires the choice-of- foreign-forum clause to be in writing. Article 63(3) further allows courts to ex officio disregard a choice-of-forum clause deemed abusive.

The freedom of contract to exercise this power is legitimized by Precedent (Súmula) n. 335 of the Federal Supreme Court, which provides: "Choice of forum clauses are valid for lawsuits arising from the contract". This provision is especially important regarding international agreements.

Law 14.879/2024, effective June 5, 2024, narrowed the scope of permissible forum selection in Article 63. Under the new law, contracting parties must confine their choices to jurisdictions relevant to the domicile or residence of one of the parties or the location of the obligation, except for consumer agreements when it benefits the consumer. The new law does not include intertemporal law rules, and when addressing the "location of the obligation," it does not clarify whether this includes the jurisdiction where the contract was formed and/or where it is enforceable.

The inclusion of compromissory clauses, stipulating that any resulting disputes will be resolved through arbitration, is a widespread practice in large-scale commodity trade contracts. This preference for arbitration often stems from its perceived advantages in terms of speed, cost-effectiveness, and confidentiality compared to traditional dispute settlement procedures.

Brazilian contracting parties frequently seek to designate arbitration centers outside of Europe, particularly in the United States and Asian commercial hubs like Singapore, for dispute resolution. This preference is driven by a geopolitical consideration: they perceive that European-based arbitration centers, and the arbitrators associated with them, may be more inclined to view regulations like the EUDR favourably, potentially influencing arbitral outcomes.

---

[84] Brazil (1942).

4.4.3 Applicable Law

In international commercial contracts, the selection of the applicable law is also a particularly sensitive issue. This decision is separate and distinct from determining jurisdiction, which is a preliminary step that must be resolved before the applicable law can be applied. Negotiating and agreeing upon a governing law that is acceptable to all parties involved can be complex, as each party may prefer the legal system of their own jurisdiction.

The United Nations Convention on Contracts for the International Sale of Goods (CISG),[85] to which Brazil is a party, is a common choice of law for commodity trade contracts. Major importers from Brazil are among the nearly 100 states that have adopted the CISG.

According to Brazilian law, Article 9 of the LINDB establishes that the applicable law for the qualification and governance of obligations shall be that of the jurisdiction wherein the obligation is constituted. This principle dictates that the law of the place of an obligation's formation is determinative as to its legal character and governance. Consequently, for obligations formed within Brazil, Brazilian law shall govern both procedural and substantive aspects. Conversely, obligations formed abroad shall be subject to the laws of the foreign jurisdiction. Therefore, the *lex causae*, which may be either domestic or foreign depending on the locus of the obligation's constitution, is vested with the authority to govern and determine the legal nature of said obligation.

4.4.4 Parallel Proceedings and lis pendens

Lis pendens aims to avoid the issuance of contradictory decisions and delays in the administration of justice. Referred to in the international literature as 'lis (alibi) pendens' (i.e., lawsuit pending), pending litigation is defined as the situation in which two parallel proceedings involving the same parties and the same subject matter are pending before courts of different states against the same time. Often used as a strategic tool, parallel proceedings are viewed as mostly undesirable inasmuch as they entail a duplication of resources, increase the risk of contradictory decisions, and have a potential for procedural harassment.

In Brazil, the Civil Procedure Code does not recognize parallel proceedings, or lis pendens, between foreign courts and Brazilian courts. This means that a lawsuit filed in a Brazilian court can proceed even if a similar lawsuit is pending in a foreign court.

---

[85] United Nations (1980).

4.4.5 *Current Trends in Commodity Trade Contracts*

The practice of international trade contracts, particularly those related to commodities, has undergone a significant transformation with the advent of the EUDR. A notable shift is the increased emphasis on robust compliance clauses pertaining to the EUDR. It has become common practice to extend contractual obligations throughout the entire supply chain, requiring all participants to adhere to the regulation's stringent requirements as a risk mitigating strategy.

Suppliers are now contractually obligated to provide comprehensive due diligence declarations, encompassing specific and verifiable data related to the origin and production of their commodities. This includes, but is not limited to, the disclosure of property deeds for land involved in the supply chain and documentation to demonstrate legal compliance and environmental sustainability. The concept of 'effective traceability' has become relevant, demanding that suppliers establish and maintain systems capable of tracking their products throughout the supply chain, ensuring transparency and accountability.

Furthermore, buyers, particularly importers subject to the EUDR, have adopted a more rigorous approach in their contractual relationships. Contracts are becoming increasingly stringent, incorporating provisions that mandate EUDR compliance and often granting buyers explicit rights to conduct compliance checks or audits of their suppliers' operations. This heightened scrutiny reflects the importers' need to ensure their own compliance with the EUDR and mitigate the risk of importing commodities linked to deforestation.

4.5 Scenarios and Potential Solutions

Considering the bottlenecks analysed in Chap. 2, 'litigation' risk may be divided into three levels: 'low', 'medium' and 'high'. This conceptualization does not come as a result of a specific methodology for risk measurement but is based on hypothetical scenarios originated from potential litigation cases. Here, 'litigation' specifically means the worst-case (contentious) scenario where parties are in direct conflict, leading to increased costs throughout the supply chain and non-compliance with EU and/or other countries' regulations. This scenario would effectively prevent Brazilian producers and exporters from operating under the EUDR.

'Low-risk' encompasses cases where conflict is either non-existent or infrequent and unsystematic. The dispute is limited to small-scale operational dynamics between the parties (e.g. Brazilian producers/exporters and EU buyers), but that do not result in the application of the EUDR's penalties. Low-risk cases include, inter alia, disagreements over the presentation or acceptance of due diligence documents, the delimitation of liability within a contractual chain or negotiations over the passing on of costs associated with the implementation of the EUDR.

'Medium-risk' represents a step further. It encompasses conflicts cases that may arise from violations of the EUDR, potentially leading to penalties. Cases like Oceanco's exemplify this level of risk.

Finally, 'high-risk' covers a systemic scenario, in which the implementation of the EUDR is rendered unfeasible due to the EU's non-recognition of third-country due diligence tools, documents, norms, and similar mechanisms. This involves situations where individual actors cannot effectively challenge the EUDR's application, necessitating intervention from a higher authority (typically the State).

Low-Risk

A 'low-risk' scenario involves minimal or occasional, small-scale conflicts that producers/exporters and buyers can resolve without penalties. This means that broader solutions are not necessary, as specific mechanism and procedures can be applied with more efficiency and celerity.

Accordingly, we envisage the adoption of three main mechanisms: the use of international private law and ADRs in contractual obligations; and/or grievance mechanisms as a preventive measure (e.g. by the incorporation in a company's compliance mechanism).

As a first strategy, contract drafting may provide for duties, rights and liabilities relating to the application of the EUDR. In this sense, the parties will agree on obligations and mechanisms to resolve any disputes that may come across. In addition, contracts may also include clauses for dispute resolution, specifically providing for the establishment of an ADR in the case of disputes, which forum to be adopted and other related issues.

Another strategy is to establish a 'complaint' system within a company, economic group or contractual chain. In this case, natural and legal persons may submit complaints/notification to authorities regarding potential regulatory non-conformity. Particularly, CSDDD's Article 14 provides a legal basis for the establishment of this strategy in both the EU and abroad. In the case of the EUDR, this can be further integrated with Article 31 regarding 'substantiated concerns', thus bringing a more direct relation with competent authorities.

Medium-Risk

A 'medium-risk' scenario involves conflicts stemming from EUDR violations, possibly leading to penalties. Unlike 'low-risk' scenarios, these cases require more substantial responses due to the impact of those penalties. They cover all mechanisms used in a 'low risk' scenario, but require greater enforcement power.

However, given that the conflict is still limited between specific contractual parties, the activation of the multilateral trade framework is not yet seen as one of the most efficient solutions. However, bilateral agreements can be brought into discussion either extrajudicially or through formal legal proceedings as they provide specific rules governing trade relations between contractual parties.

High-Risk

A 'high-risk' scenario implies a systemic approach in which the EU does not recognise information, documents, norms and other mechanisms adopted by the countries of origin. In this sense, not just a single operation is affected, but the entire relationship between a third country and an EU member.

To bring potential solutions to this scenario, a more holistic approach should be favoured. Thus, we envisage the use of (1) bilateral agreements, as consensual mechanisms between parties and with their own delineated dynamics; or (2) trade-related mechanisms, such as the WTO's system and the MPIA. This does not mean, however, that the other mechanisms might not be applicable, but their potential for a more holistic solution to the dispute falls short.

Bilateral agreements, such as the EU-Mercosur, can provide specific rules that may 'override' the provisions of the EUDR. Even more, the chapter on trade and sustainable development (TSD) and its dispute settlement mechanisms can provide tools to both solve conflict cases and to address dialogues between the agreement's parties. In this case, a tangible solution is to foster the mutual recognition of mechanisms under the scope of the Agreement and to enforce its implementation, thus creating and ensuring that all parties comply with the set of rules consensually agreed.

On the other hand, dispute can also be taken to the WTO. This requires demonstrating a clear inconsistency between the EU norm and the GATT framework and other WTO regulations. WTO case law, as developed in cases DS 600 and DS 593, establishes that the complainant bears the burden of proof in demonstrating a violation of WTO rules by third parties. In such cases, the WTO has understood the EU's MBMs were consistent with WTO's rules as Indonesia and Malaysia failed to prove otherwise. However, both DS 600 and 593 rulings recognize the need for the implementation of EU norms to respect the international trade regime. Thus, cases brought to the WTO must consider both the incompatibility of the EUDR itself and its implementation with the WTO framework.

Due to the 'freezing' of the WTO, the MPIA has currently become a more attractive alternative. Recognized on the basis of Article 25 of the DSU, the mechanism allows both MPIA members and non-members to join. Moreover, the procedure can even be adopted after a WTO's panel is initiated (but before the panel report is circulated). The implementation of the MPIA in a dispute settlement involves the inclusion of an appeal arbitration agreement when establishing the Dispute Settlement Panel. Therefore, as in the cases of the ADR mechanisms, fostering the inclusion of arbitration agreements in international fora may present a good strategy to provide alternatives applicable under international trade rules.

4.6 Section Conclusion

Given the intersection of the EUDR with international trade, and considering the bottlenecks identified in the previous Chapter, there is a risk that potential conflicts will arise from the implementation of the norm. Considering this, players may take into account some measures to prevent or mitigate conflict scenarios.

In cases of no conflict (such as in a prevention scenario) or small-scale disputes (punctual disagreements), players may: (i) implement preventive contractual measures, such as specific clauses that explicitly outline the due diligence obligations of each stakeholder involved in the transaction or that mandate the verification of commodity origin and legality; (ii) implement legal procedures for seamless information sharing and collaboration among all supply chain participants; (iii) provide for periodic audits and assessments to monitor compliance and proactively identify potential risks; (iv) defineand implement clear and enforceable penalties for non-compliance; and (v) carefully draft multi-tier dispute resolution clauses in contracts.

In cases of medium-scale conflicts (those that may lead to factual judicial conflicts or effectively impact trade relations, such as contract termination), players may: (i) Renegotiate existing contracts to achieve EUDR compliance, aiming for mutually beneficial outcomes; (ii) activate the initial phase of multi-tier dispute resolution clauses (as recommended in the previous scenario), prioritizing mediation and other alternative dispute resolution mechanisms; (iii) enforce existing contractual provisions where applicable, including activating non-performance clauses, pursuing penalty claims, and issuing extrajudicial warnings regarding potential litigation; (iv) proceed with litigation through arbitration or judicial enforcement as stipulated in the contract; and (v) Engage political consultation mechanisms as outlined in bilateral trade agreements to facilitate non-adjudicative resolution of disagreements and foster collaborative solutions. Bilateral agreements can also offer other mechanisms that can guide partners to potential solutions concerning EUDR related issues.

For large-scale conflicts, which may encompass the interference of government and other State representatives, players may: (i) formally question the legality of the EUDR with respect to the international trade framework governed by the WTO. This should include pursuing a dispute through the WTO Dispute Settlement Body; (ii) as an alternative or in conjunction with the formal WTO dispute process, pursue dispute resolution through the MPIA.

References

AF&PA et al (2024) Global forest-based industries' call for legal clarity and adequate transition time to ensure a smooth and effective implementation of the EU Deforestation Regulation. https://d4d14e3d-083d-4afc-807e-788bd740bca8.filesusr.com/ugd/d13736_babe73c14ca74f3ab46b98dbd0cbdaf8.pdf. Accessed 22 Dec 2024

Amigos da Terra et al (2023) Joint letter of civil society organisations working in non-EU countries. https://amigosdaterra.org.br/wp-content/uploads/2023/12/Joint-letter-EUDR-12.12.NEW-1.pdf. Accessed 22 Dec 2024

APIB et al (2024) Every second counts to protect global forests and ecosystems. https://www.oc.eco.br/wp-content/uploads/2024/05/Every-second-counts-Letter-to-UVDL-on-EUDR.pdf. Accessed 22 Dec 2024

Associação Brasileira do Agronegócio [ABAG] (2023) Associação de agronegócio do Brasil reage contra lei da UE sobre desmatamento. https://abag.com.br/associacao-de-agronegocio-do-brasil-reage-contra-lei-da-ue-sobre-desmatamento/. Accessed 22 Dec 2024

Bataier C (2024) Organizations criticize the postponement of the EU anti-deforestation law and mention agribusiness lobby. https://www.brasildefato.com.br/2024/10/04/organizations-criticize-the-postponement-of-the-eu-anti-deforestation-law-and-mention-agribusiness-lobby. Accessed 16 Jan 2025

Bioenergy Europe et al (2024) EUDR information system not yet on track to meet requirements of properly functioning supply chains. https://fefac.eu/newsroom/news/eudr-information-system-not-yet-on-track-to-meet-requirements-of-properly-functioning-supply-chains/. Accessed 22 Dec 2024

Brazil (1942) Law-Decree n.º 4.657/1942. https://www.planalto.gov.br/ccivil_03/decreto-lei/del4657compilado.htm. Accessed 22 Nov 2024

Brazil (2015) Federal Law n.º 13.105/2015. https://www.planalto.gov.br/ccivil_03/_ato2015-2018/2015/lei/l13105.htm. Accessed 20 Nov 2024

Brazil (2024) Comexstat. https://comexstat.mdic.gov.br/pt/home. Accessed 29 May 2025

Buysing Damsté C et al (2024) How the EU's Green Deal is driving business reinvention. https://www.pwc.com/gx/en/issues/esg/eu-green-deal-reinvention.html. Accessed 22 Dec 2024

Canfin P (2025) Post on LinkedIn. https://www.linkedin.com/posts/pascal-canfin_a-fake-consultation-on-the-omnibus-the-european-activity-7292238177539358721-8dFu/?utm_source=share&utm_medium=member_android. Accessed 17 Jan 2025

Charnovitz S (1997) The world trade organization and the environment. Yearb Int Environ Law 8:98–116. https://charnovitz.org/publications/The_World_Trade_Organization_and_the_Environment.pdf. Accessed 28 May 2025

Confederação Nacional de Indústrias (2023) Regulamento da União Europeia condiciona importação de determinadas commodities agrícolas e seus derivados a due diligence de desmatamento. Política Comercial n.º 10, 2023. https://static.portaldaindustria.com.br/media/filer_public/78/99/78990af4-d034-4897-8013-252abe5b3ec2/apc_regulamento_ue_desmatamento_ano_2_n_10.pdf. Accessed 22 Dec 2024

Congressional Research Service (2024) Implications of the European Union Deforestation Regulation. https://crsreports.congress.gov/product/pdf/IF/IF12777. Accessed 15 Jan 2025

Council of the European Union (2024) Urgent call for action: challenges for European agriculture and forestry businesses posed by the Deforestation Regulation in the context of the current agricultural crisis. https://www.parlament.gv.at/gegenstand/XXVII/EU/178105?selectedStage=100. Accessed 22 Dec 2024

Dobson N (2023) Climate protection versus trade: dilemmas for the EU. In: Handbook on European Union climate change policy and politics. Edward Elgar Publishing, pp 367–382

EU cross-commodity coalition on EUDR implementation (2024) Joint cross-commodity call to EU Commission and Member States to provide urgent clarifications and workable solutions for EUDR implementation. https://www.coceral.com/data/1711704766President%20Khattabi-Joint%20cross%20sector%20coalition%20letter%20on%20EUDR%20implementation.pdf. Accessed 22 Dec 2024

EUR-Lex (2020) Regulation (EU) 2020/852 of the European Parliament and of the Council of 18 June 2020 on the establishment of a framework to facilitate sustainable investment, and amending Regulation (EU) 2019/2088. https://eur-lex.europa.eu/eli/reg/2020/852/oj/eng. Accessed 22 Dec 2024

EUR-Lex (2022) Directive (EU) 2022/2464 of the European Parliament and of the Council of 14 December 2022 amending Regulation (EU) No 537/2014, Directive 2004/109/EC, Directive 2006/43/EC and Directive 2013/34/EU, as regards corporate sustainability reporting. https://eur-lex.europa.eu/eli/dir/2022/2464/oj/eng. Accessed 22 Dec 2024

EUR-Lex (2024a) Directive (EU) 2024/1760 of the European Parliament and of the Council of 13 June 2024 on corporate sustainability due diligence and amending Directive (EU) 2019/1937 and Regulation (EU) 2023/2859. https://eur-lex.europa.eu/eli/dir/2024/1760/oj/eng. Accessed 05 Jan 2025

EUR-Lex (2024b) Commission Notice – Guidance document for Regulation (EU) 2023/1115 on deforestation-free products. https://eur-lex.europa.eu/legal-content/EN/TXT/?uri=CELEX%3A52024XC06789&qid=1731687748447. Accessed 06 Dec 2024

European Commission (2024a) Directive on corporate sustainability due diligence frequently asked questions. https://finance.ec.europa.eu/document/download/c4e40e92-8633-4bda-97cf-0af13e70bc3f_en?filename=240807-faqs-corporate-sustainability-reporting_en.pdf. Accessed 29 May 2025

European Commission (2024b) EUDR - Myths vs. Reality. https://green-business.ec.europa.eu/deforestation-regulation-implementation/eudr-myth-buster_en. Accessed 22 Dec 2024

European Commission. EU-Chile text of the agreement. https://circabc.europa.eu/ui/group/09242a36-a438-40fd-a7af-fe32e36cbd0e/library/7668ad45-b14f-4ef6-823d-8899fbac72d2/details?download=true. Accessed 30 April 2025

European Council (2023) Corporate sustainability due diligence: Council and Parliament strike deal to protect environment and human rights. https://www.consilium.europa.eu/en/press/press-releases/2023/12/14/corporate-sustainability-due-diligence-council-and-parliament-strike-deal-to-protect-environment-and-human-rights/. Accessed 22 Dec 2024

European Union. EU-Singapore: texts of the agreements. https://policy.trade.ec.europa.eu/eu-trade-relationships-country-and-region/countries-and-regions/singapore/eu-singapore-agreements/texts-agreements_en. Accessed 30 April 2025

Fern (2020) The EU-Mercosur Trade Agreement Explainer. https://www.fern.org/fileadmin/uploads/fern/Documents/2020/The_EU-Mercosur_Trade_Agreement_explainer.pdf. Accessed 28 April 2025

GlobalData (2024) EUDR could cost EU consumers up to $1.5 billion, as new sustainability rules set to impact global commodity supply chains, says new GlobalData study. https://www.globaldata.com/custom-solutions/solutions-in-action/eudr-cost-eu-consumers-1-5-billion-new-sustainability-rules-set-impact-global-commodity-supply-chains-says-new-study/?. Accessed 22 Dec 2024

Government of Canada, Text of the Comprehensive and Economic Agreement (CETA). https://www.international.gc.ca/trade-commerce/assets/pdfs/ceta-rm-01-eng.pdf. Accessed 29 April 2025

Gstohl S, Schnock J (2024) Towards a coherent trade-environment nexus? The EU's critical raw materials policy. J World Trade 58(1):35–60

International Trade Centre (2024) Trade Map. https://www.trademap.org/Country_SelProduct.aspx?nvpm=1%7c%7c%7c%7c%7c1801%7c%7c%7c4%7c1%7c1%7c2%7c1%7c1%7c2%7c1%7c1%7c1. Accessed 28 Feb 2024

Johnston C, Guo J, Prestemon J (2025) The European union deforestation regulation: implications for the global forest sector. Forest Policy Econ 173. https://doi.org/10.1016/j.forpol.2025.103462

Kommerkollegium (2024) The cumulative effect of EU regulations on external trade. https://www.kommerskollegium.se/globalassets/publikationer/rapporter/2024/cumulative-effect-regulations-external-trade.pdf. Accessed 19 Jan 2025

Koul A (2018) Guide to WTO and GATT: economics, law and politics, 6th edn. Springer Nature Singapore Pte Ltd

Marín Durán G, Scott J (2022) Regulating trade in forest-risk commodities: two cheers for the european union. J Environ Law 34(2):245–267

Matsushita M et al (2015) The world trade organization: law, practice, and policy, 3rd edn. Oxford University Press

Nabeshima K, Obashi A (2021) Impact of regulatory burdens on international trade. J Japan Int Econ 59. https://doi.org/10.1016/j.jjie.2020.101120

Pauwelyn J (2023) The MPIA: What's New? https://ielp.worldtradelaw.net/2023/02/the-mpia-whats-new-part-ii.html. Accessed 30 May 2025

Pelc K (2024) Have WTO members successfully circumvented the US' blockade of the appellate body? (and How Would We Know?). https://www.ejiltalk.org/have-wto-members-successfully-circumvented-the-us-blockade-of-the-appellate-body-and-how-would-we-know/. Accessed 30 May 2025

Proforest (2025) Webinar EUDR – Dry runs for beef and soy supply chains in 4 Mercosur countries. https://www.youtube.com/watch?v=-Q6W9mtHs60. Accessed 22 Mar 2025

Profundo (2025) Analysis of EUDR compliance costs. https://profundo.nl/projects/analysis-of-eudr-compliance-costs-/. Accessed 20 Feb 2025

Read R (2005) Process and production methods and the regulation of international trade. In: The WTO and the regulation of international trade. https://www.oas.org/dsd/tool-kit/Documentos/ModuleIIIdoc/Read%20Article%20on%20PPMs.pdf. Accessed 20 Mar 2025

Reuters (2023) Indonesia accuses EU of 'regulatory imperialism' with deforestation law. https://www.reuters.com/business/environment/indonesia-accuses-eu-regulatory-imperialism-with-deforestation-law-2023-06-08/. Accessed 30 May 2025

Senado (2025) Senado aprova Lei da Reciprocidade Econômica. https://www12.senado.leg.br/institucional/presidencia/noticia/davi-alcolumbre/senado-aprova-lei-da-reciprocidade-economica-1. Accessed 29 May 2025

Shukla A (2024) The future of trade and environment: a roadmap for reconciling two competing goals. J World Trade 58(1):115–130

Sikora I, Sela S (2024) Chart: the impact of the EU's deforestation regulation, from coffee to cattle. https://blogs.worldbank.org/en/trade/chart--the-impact-of-the-eu-s-deforestation-regulation--from-cof. Accessed 22 Dec 2024

United Kingdom National Archives (2021) Environment Act 2021

United Nations Trade and Development (2021) More than 100 countries depend on commodity exports. https://unctad.org/news/more-100-countries-depend-commodity-exports#:~:text=Commodity%20dependence%20increased%20over%20the,report%20released%20on%208%20September. Accessed 31 May 2024

United Nations (1980) United Nations Convention on Contracts for the International Sale of Goods

United States Congress (2023) S.3371 — 118th Congress (2023–2024). https://www.congress.gov/bill/118th-congress/senate-bill/3371/text. Accessed 30 May 2025

Unites States Senate (2024) Urgent Call For Action: challenges for European agriculture and forestry businesses posed by the Deforestation Regulation in the context of the current agricultural crisis. https://www.parlament.gv.at/gegenstand/XXVII/EU/178105?selectedStage=100. Accessed 22 Dec 2024

Vij V (2023) Changing realities: evolution and extraterritoriality within Article XX(G) of GATT for global environmental concerns. Trade L Dev 14(2):195–238

Walk Free (2025) Thailand to introduce mandatory supply chain due diligence law. https://www.walkfree.org/news/2025/thailand-to-introduce-mandatory-supply-chain-due-diligence-law/. Accessed 15 Mar 2025

World Trade Organization (WTO). Marrakesh Agreement 1994. https://www.wto.org/english/docs_e/legal_e/04-wto_e.htm. Accessed 22 Feb 2024

World Trade Organization (1994a) US—Restrictions on Imports of Tuna Dolphin I, GATT B.I.S.D. (39th Supp.) at 155; US—Restrictions on Imports of Tuna Dolphin II, DS29/R, 16 June 1994, reprinted in 33 I.L.M. 839

World Trade Organization (1994b) US—Restrictions on Imports of Tuna Dolphin I, GATT B.I.S.D. (39th Supp.) at 155; US—Restrictions on Imports of Tuna Dolphin II, DS29/R, 16 June 1994, reprinted in 33 I.L.M. 839 (1994) (unadopted)

World Trade Organization (1995) DS2: United States — Standards for Reformulated and Conventional Gasoline. https://www.wto.org/english/tratop_e/dispu_e/cases_e/ds2_e.htm. Accessed 22 Dec 2024

World Trade Organization (1996a) DS58: United States — Import Prohibition of Certain Shrimp and Shrimp Products. https://www.wto.org/english/tratop_e/dispu_e/cases_e/ds58_e.htm. Accessed 22 Dec 2024

World Trade Organization (1996b) DS58: United States — Import Prohibition of Certain Shrimp and Shrimp Products. https://www.wto.org/english/tratop_e/dispu_e/cases_e/ds58_e.htm. Accessed 22 Dec 2024

World Trade Organization (2004) Trade and Environment at the WTO. https://www.wto.org/english/tratop_e/envir_e/envir_wto2004_e.pdf. Accessed 20 Dec 2024
World Trade Organization (2005) DS332: Brazil — Measures Affecting Imports of Retreaded Tyres. https://www.wto.org/english/tratop_e/dispu_e/cases_e/ds332_e.htm. Accessed 22 Dec 2024
World Trade Organization (2019a) DS591: Colombia — Anti-Dumping Duties on Frozen Fries from Belgium, Germany and the Netherlands. https://www.wto.org/english/tratop_e/dispu_e/cases_e/ds591_e.htm. Accessed 05 Jan 2025
World Trade Organization (2019b) DS583: Turkey - Certain Measures Concerning the Production, Importation and Marketing of Pharmaceutical Products
World Trade Organization (2022a) Trade Policy Review Body. Trade Policy Review Report: Brazil (WT/TPR/S/432/Rev.1). https://docs.wto.org/dol2fe/Pages/SS/directdoc.aspx?filename=q:/WT/TPR/S432R1.pdf&Open=True. Accessed 27 May 2025
World Trade Organization. Committee on Agriculture (2022b, Nov 29) Joint letter submitted by Indonesia and Brazil. https://docs.wto.org/dol2fe/Pages/SS/directdoc.aspx?filename=q:/G/AG/GEN213.pdf&Open=True. Accessed 22 Dec 2024
World Trade Organization (2022c) WT/CTE/29
World Trade Organization (2023a) WT/GC/W/912. https://docs.wto.org/dol2fe/Pages/SS/directdoc.aspx?filename=q:/WT/GC/W912.pdf&Open=True. Accessed 22 Dec 2024
World Trade Organization (2023b) WT/GC/W912
World Trade Organization (2023c) WT/CTE/GEN/33
World Trade Organization (2024a) DS600: European Union and certain Member states — Certain Measures Concerning Palm Oil and Oil Palm Crop-Based Biofuels. https://www.wto.org/english/tratop_e/dispu_e/cases_e/ds600_e.htm. Accessed 22 Dec 2024
World Trade Organization (2024b) Appellate Body. https://www.wto.org/english/tratop_e/dispu_e/appellate_body_e.htm#:~:text=The%20Appellate%20Body%20can%20uphold,its%20seat%20in%20Geneva%2C%20Switzerland. Accessed 22 Dec 2024
World Trade Organization (2024c) Committee on Trade and Environment. https://www.wto.org/english/tratoP_e/envir_e/wrk_committee_e.htm. Accessed 22 Dec 2024
World Trade Organization (2024d) Understanding on rules and procedures governing the settlement of disputes. https://www.wto.org/english/tratop_e/dispu_e/dsu_e.htm. Accessed 22 Dec 2024
World Trade Organization (2024e) Environmental Database. https://edb.wto.org/. Accessed 30 May 2025
World Trade Organization (2024f) WT/CTE/31
World Trade Organization (2025) DS593: European Union — Certain Measures Concerning Palm Oil and Oil Palm Crop-Based Biofuels. https://www.wto.org/english/tratop_e/dispu_e/cases_e/ds593_e.htm. Accessed 20 Jan 2025
World Trade Organization. Short Answers to Big Questions on the WTO and the Environment. https://www.wto.org/english/res_e/booksp_e/envirqapublication_e.pdf. Accessed 22 Dec 2024
World Trade Organization Plurilaterals (2025)
WWF (2024a) The impacts of European Union Deforestation Regulation (EUDR) on Chinese forest companies and policy recommendation. https://forestsolutions.panda.org/uploads/default/report/The_impacts_of_EUDR_on_Chinese_forest_companies_and_policy_recommendations.pdf. Accessed 15 Jan 2025
WWF (2024b) WWF launches EUDR Step-by-step Guide for Business. https://forestsforward.panda.org/?14709791/WWF-launches-EUDR-guide-for-business. Accessed 29 May 2025
Ziegler A (2025) On 10 January, the WTO circulated a panel report in the case brought by Indonesia concerning EU measures affecting palm oil and biofuels (DS 593). https://intlawch.wordpress.com/2025/01/19/on-10-january-the-wto-circulated-a-panel-report-in-the-case-brought-by-indonesia-concerning-eu-measures-affecting-palm-oil-and-biofuels-ds-593/. Accessed 25 Jan 2025

Chapter 5
The Impacts of the EUDR in Brazil

5.1 Brazilian Forest-Related Framework

Brazilian current environmental protection framework was not fully structured until the second half of the twentieth century. Since the 1930s, the country had only sectoral regulatory frameworks, which were not part of a larger, integrated environmental policy.[1] Although a major step for the protection of forests and the environment in general, the 1934 Forest Code (Decree 23.793/1934)[2] and its 1965 revised version (Law 4.771/65)[3] lacked in enforcement mechanisms. Shortly after the influence of the 1972 Stockholm Conference, Brazilian Special Secretariat for the Environment (SEMA)[4] was created as the first federal agency specialized in dealing with environmental issues. It was then followed, in 1981, by the establishment of the National Environmental Policy (Law 6.938/81)[5] and the National Environmental System (SISNAMA),[6] composed by the National Council for the Environment (CONAMA)[7] as a collegiate body.

The 1988 Federal Constitution[8] of Brazil has dedicated a specific section to address environmental issues. Article 225 of the Constitution protects the right of everyone to an 'ecologically balanced environment', which is 'essential for a healthy life'. The Article states that the Government and the community have a duty to defend and to preserve the environment for present and future generations. Paragraph 4 of Article 225 establishes the biomes Amazon Forest, Atlantic Forest and Pantanal

[1] Moura (2016).
[2] Brazil (1934).
[3] Brazil (1965).
[4] Brazil (1973).
[5] Brazil (1981).
[6] Brazil (2024).
[7] MMA. 'CONAMA'.
[8] Brazil (1988).

P. Wojcikiewicz Almeida et al., *The Normative and Regulatory Challenges for the Implementation of the European Deforestation-Free Regulation in Third Affected Countries*, https://doi.org/10.1007/978-3-032-08458-3_5

as national heritage. Thus, specific legislation was created to manage them. For instance, the 1988 Constitution reinstated the right of the States, Federal District and Municipalities to legislate complementarily to the Federal Government about forestry matters (Articles 23 and 24).

The current 2012 Forest Code is the main legal instrument for regulating land use on private rural lands in Brazil.[9] The Forest Code establishes general rules for the protection of vegetation, especially 'Permanent Preservation Areas' (APPs) and 'Legal Reserves' (RLs). Legal Reserves are portions of land that must be set aside in native habitat, depending on property size and location—this protected percentage varies from 20 to 80% depending on the type of vegetation present and the property's geographical location. Permanent Preservation Areas are protected areas, covered by native vegetation or not, with special environmental functions, such as facilitate genetic flows of fauna and flora, protect the soil, and ensure human wellbeing.

The 2012 Forest Code also regulates forest exploitation, the supply of forest raw materials, the control of the origin of forest products, and the control and prevention of forest fires. It recognizes that the forests and other forms of native vegetation existing in the national territory, recognized as useful to the lands they cover, are assets of common interest to all inhabitants of the country. Property rights over these areas are limited by the legislation in general and especially by the Forest Code.

The new Forest Code also introduced an innovative database called the 'Rural Environmental Registry' (Cadastro Ambiental Rural, or CAR), which provides georeferenced data on private properties.[10] It integrates the environmental information of the rural properties for more effective management and planning in rural areas. It also serves as a tool to monitor and control deforestation in private landholdings. Landowners must register in the CAR in order to exercise several rights in the Forest Code, such as obtaining authorization to remove native vegetation, accessing benefits granted to landowners who illegally cleared forest prior to July 2008, and accessing rural credit from financial institutions.

The tool includes data from the owner, rural possessor or directly responsible for the rural property, the georeferenced plan of the perimeter of the property, areas of social interest and areas of public utility, with information on the location of the remaining native vegetation, areas of permanent preservation, areas of restricted use, consolidated areas and the location of legal reserves. Registration in the CAR is mandatory for all rural properties and possessions in the country and is declaratory and permanent in nature. The registration of the rural property in the CAR is carried out through an electronic system and is carried out with the competent state body, in the Federation Unit (UF) where the rural property is located. At the federal level, the Brazilian Forest Service (SFB) is responsible for coordinating registration and providing technical support for its implementation in federative entities, through the provision of technological solutions.

The CAR, however, may face some criticism. For instance, as the submitted information is self-declared, public authorities must analyse the veracity and adequacy of

[9] Brazil (2012).

[10] Brazil (2024).

the information. That is, the CAR becomes active immediately after the registration in its system, regardless of prior assessment of its veracity.

The 2012 Forest Code offers additional tools for rural landowners. The 'Environmental Regularization Program' (in Portuguese, Programa de Regularização Ambiental), which comprises a set of actions and initiatives that must be developed by landowners to adjust and promote the environmental regularization of their land. 'Environmental Reserve Quotas' (in Portuguese, Cotas de Reserva Ambiental) are certificates that represent a portion of an area of natural vegetation cover on a property that can be used to compensate for the lack of a Legal Reserve on another property.

In addition, as part of the implementation of the revised Forest Code, in 2017 Brazil launched SINAFLOR[11]—the 'National System for Controlling the Origin of Forest Products' from source to sale. SINAFLOR seeks to integrate the federal electronic traceability system for timber—known as 'Declarations of Forest Origin' (in Portuguese, Declaração de Origem Florestal).

Forest conservation in public areas is carried out through the 'National System of Conservation Units' (in Portuguese, Sistema Nacional de Unidades de Conservação da Natureza), abbreviated SNUC, created by Law 9.985/2000.[12] It comprises a set of regulations that enable the federal, state and municipal government departments, as well as private initiative, to create, implement and manage 'Conservation Units' (UC). UCs are protected areas with relevant natural features, which have among their purposes the preservation, sustainable use, and restoration of natural environments, including forestry. Brazil currently has a total of 2,376 UCs, including federal, state, and municipal units, which cover about 18% of the country's territory and 26% of its marine areas. These units are divided into two main types—full protection and sustainable use—and subdivided into a dozen different categories.

Law 11.284/2006 regulates public forests management with the view of granting sustainable timber production.[13] Special attention is devoted to local community management, forest concessions, environmental licensing and forestry prices. Moreover, it institutes, within the Ministry for Environment and Climate Change, the SFB and the National Fund for Forestry Development (FNDF). The legislation provides also a classification of municipal, State or federal forests. Finally, it rules on the bodies in charge for forestry management and monitoring. Thus, Law 11.284/2006 is not only closely related to the 2012 Forest Code, but also to the National System of Conservation Units, integrating the forest protection microsystem.

Brazil has an extensive policy framework regulating its forests. At the federal level, the forest management is under the direct responsibility of four institutions. The Ministry of the Environment and Climate Change (often abbreviated as MMA) is responsible for formulating forestry policies. It operates by granting power for sustainable forest production and is responsible for signing forest concession contracts. The SFB is the administrative institution of the federal public forests for the sustainable production of goods and services. It is also responsible for the generation

[11] Brazilian Institute of the Environment and Renewable Natural Resources (2024).

[12] Brazil (2000).

[13] Brazil (2006).

of information, qualifications, and fostering the forest area. The Brazilian Institute of the Environment and of Renewable Natural Resources (IBAMA) is the institution responsible for environmental control and inspection, and is also responsible for licensing and environmental control of the Brazilian forests in its area of competence. The Institute Chico Mendes of Conservation and Biodiversity (ICMBio) is responsible for proposing, implementing, managing, protecting, inspecting, and monitoring the Conservation Units instituted by the Federal Government.

Additionally, the federal government, spanning through different administrations, has implemented key policies to address illegal deforestation. Between the late 1980s and the 1990s, the migration trends and disorderly land occupation led to the deforestation of approximately 18 million hectares in the Amazon region, reaching its peak in 1995.

Faced with this scenario, Brazil adopted in 2004 the 'Action Plan for the Prevention and Control of Deforestation in the Legal Amazon' (in Portuguese, Plano de Ação para Prevenção e Controle do Desmatamento da Amazônia Legal—PPCDAM)[14] with the goal of combatting deforestation and promoting sustainable development in the Legal Amazon. The Plan ushered in a new era of rainforest protection through a multi-level approach. This included real-time deforestation monitoring via advanced satellite technology; prioritized intervention in municipalities experiencing recent deforestation; conditional access to subsidized rural credit, requiring compliance with environmental regulations.

PPCDAM's first three phases were largely successful, as they contributed to a reduction of over 80% in the annual deforestation rate in the Amazon between 2004 and 2012.[15] Building upon the success of the PPCDAM, the Brazilian government extended this approach to other biomes through the 'Cerrado Action Plan' (PPCerrado) launched in 2010, specifically targeting the protection of the Cerrado biome; and the 'Environmental Monitoring Program for Brazilian Biomes' (PMABB) established in 2015, providing a comprehensive monitoring framework for all Brazilian biomes.

After a few years of increased deforestation rates, the government implemented the fifth phase of PPCDAM in 2023, with a target of zero deforestation by 2030, and has recently launched a new phase of PPCerrado. The Brazilian government's renewed efforts to curb deforestation in the Amazon are already showing results. From January to July 2023, there was a 42% decrease in deforestation in the region compared to the same period the previous year.

Brazil has revitalized multi-stakeholder consultations on deforestation and climate change, signaling a renewed commitment to collaboration after a period of reduced engagement on both executive and legislative fronts.

Established in 2015, the 'National REDD+ Committee' (CONAREDD+)[16] was reinstated in 2023 to coordinate the national REDD+ strategy (framework to protect forests as part of the Paris Agreement). It brings together representatives from various

---

[14] Brazil. Ministério do Meio Ambiente e Mudança do Clima (MMA).

[15] Ibid.

[16] Brazil (2024).

government levels (ministries, state governments, municipalities) alongside civil society organizations. CONAREDD+ can also establish temporary expert panels to address specific themes related to deforestation and climate change. The resumption also strengthens the Amazon Fund, the largest REDD+ mechanism on the planet.

The 'Permanent Parliamentary Joint Commission on Climate Change', which operates within the National Congress, serves as a platform for discussing and monitoring climate change issues in Brazil. It facilitates public consultations and hearings, fostering public participation and holding the executive branch accountable for its actions on climate change.

In terms of business operations, Brazil has established a three-phase environmental licensing system[17] (prior licence, installation licence and operating licence). In this system, there is public participation throughout the process by various means, such as public hearings, technical information meetings and public consultations, in accordance with the legislation.

In addition, both Brazilian and private entities have developed a series of mechanisms in order to implement the forest-related framework. This includes certifications, monitoring and traceability systems, labelling, and special programs to combat deforestation and other environmental challenges. For instance, National Council of Justice (CNJ) Recommendation No. 145/2023[18] recommends the use of remote sensing data and information obtained by satellite for environmental actions, which includes monitoring Mechanisms such as PRODES, DETER-B, Mapbiomas Alerta, Brasil MAIS, GLAD, JJ-FAST, SAD Imazon and SIPAMSAR.

In terms of monitoring systems, TerraBrasilis is a platform developed by INPE that organizes and provides access, through a web portal, to geographic data produced by INPE on the transformations occurring in terms of land cover and use in the country. The tool is a spatial data analysis infrastructure, based on complex algorithms, which provides interfaces that are not only found in traditional geographic information systems. With cutting-edge technologies, the system was developed to guarantee the best performance, allow high availability, smaller size, simplicity to produce increments, reliability for changes and fault tolerance in unstable computer network scenarios, to adjust to the input format of complex algorithms and to speed up the loading of the web application so that it is faster than other systems.

The platform follows international standards for the dissemination of geographic data and the specifications of the National Spatial Data Infrastructure (INDE). This makes the data produced interoperable, that is, it can be part of other visualization and analysis platforms. Furthermore, TerraBrasilis provides an interactive panel where users can interact with different types of graphics that summarize the information generated to facilitate understanding.

The images produced by INPE and published on the TerraBrasilis platform serve as a basis for government environmental monitoring programs such as the Deforestation in the Legal Amazon Satellite Project (PRODES) and the Deforestation Detection System in Real Time (DETER). PRODES and DETER demonstrated their

[17] Brazil (2011).

[18] Conselho Nacional de Justiça. Protocolo para Julgamento de Ações Ambientais (2023).

commitment to monitoring the mapping of large-scale deforestation areas systematically and through data quality assurance. The complexity of the programs requires the design, implementation and deployment of a spatial data infrastructure based on extensive data analysis features. And this is what INPE, through TerraBrasilis, provides for these programs.

However, the DETER project has shown limited results in tracking the recent changes in deforestation trends, as they have reduced in overall size. Thus, to assist in monitoring this new pattern, the DETER-B project was created, as it identifies and maps, in near real time, deforestation with a minimum area close to 1 hectare. For this, images from the WFI sensors of the CBERS-4 satellite (Sino-Brazilian Land Resources Satellite) and AWiFS of the IRS satellite (Indian Remote Sensing Satellite) are used. Additionally, the TerraClass project was reinstated in 2023, a partnership between INPE and Embrapa that aims to produce systemic maps of land use for deforested areas in the Legal Amazon.

MapBiomas is another technological-informational instrument built by a collaborative network, formed by NGOs, universities and technology startups, which, in a similar way to TerraBrasilis, aims to reveal the transformations of the Brazilian territory, with precision, agility and quality, in order to make knowledge about the coverage and use of Brazilian land accessible and, in this way, contribute to the conservation of natural resources and the fight against climate change.

MapBiomas covers data since 1985 on deforestation, regeneration, forest fires, water levels and cultivation areas. To monitor these transformations in land use, MapBiomas digitally divided the region into 9.6 billion squares of equal size and made them available on its digital platform. It is no surprise that the organization is responsible for validating and preparing reports for each deforestation event detected in Brazil since January 2019. It is also worth remembering that MapBiomas is also present throughout Latin America, covering a series of topics related to various countries, such as mining and agriculture.

Regarding traceability, Brazil has different mechanisms to track its supply chain. The Brazilian government agency Embrapa developed, in 2022, the 'Brazilian Agro-Traceability System' (SIBRAAR) that tracks agro-industrial products, offering information about their quality and origin, in a transparent and reliable way, using digital blockchain technology. The system is aimed at the agroindustry and can be customized for application in derivatives of various agricultural crops. Based on this system, the consumer, through a QR Code printed on the packaging, has direct access to information about the product: from the rural property where it originated, through the processing stages to its distribution and commercialization on the market.

Furthermore, the Brazilian federal government launched the 'Brazilian Cattle and Buffalo Individual Identification System' (SISBOV), an individual cattle identification system. It aims to register and identify the cattle and buffalo herd in the national territory in order to enable the tracking of animals from birth to slaughter, thus providing support for decision-making relating the quality of national herd and imported. In this system, adherence by rural producers is voluntary, except when its obligation is defined in a specific normative act, or required by official health controls or programs. Also, the 'Animal Transit Guide' (GTA) provide data essential for domestic and international trade.

Lastly, the 'AgroBrasil + Sustentável' platform project[19] is a voluntary, universal and free digital government tool that is expected to provide organised, traceable and reliable information on sustainable agricultural production. The initiative has been praised by Brazilian stakeholders and may contribute to the EUDR's compliance. However, it still was in its early stages by January 2025.

In terms of rastreability and certification, Brazilian mechanism are divided into general and commodity-specific tools. As a broad initiative, Brazil issued the 'Selo Verde Brasil'[20] (Federal Decree No. 12.063/2024), with the objective to develop national (voluntary) guidelines for the standardization and certification of products to meet sustainability requirements.

The Program also aims to reduce the multitude of environmental requirements that apply to Brazilian products. In this way, it aims to unify the various Brazilian environmental labelling initiatives established by governmental and private entities. Furthermore, it intends to harmonize the requirements established by governments and private entities from third countries, compliance with which conditions access to the market for Brazilian products and services abroad. The Brazil Green Seal Program aims to help Brazilian exporters to prove compliance with environmental norms and regulations in the main international markets, which will contribute to reducing bureaucracy and reducing costs for the exporter. It is then considered the "export passport" of national producers.

Any products and services originating from the primary, secondary or tertiary sectors of the national economy and that meet the sustainability criteria defined within the scope of the Program can receive the Brazil Green Seal. As of voluntary participation, it can be obtained by legal entities accredited by INMETRO (an institution that has formal recognition of competence for inspection or certification in Brazil) to carry out conformity assessment tasks, according to established requirements. In this way, the program is able to convey confidence to the buyer and the regulatory authority, thus facilitating trade across borders.

On the other hand, a notorious regional certification body is 'Selo Verde de Minas Gerais' (Green Seal-MG). The Green Seal-MG is a platform developed by researchers of the University of Minas Gerais (UFMG), in partnership with the Government of Minas Gerais and the Territorial Intelligence Center, and support from the AL-INVEST Verde program of the EU. It offers individualized information on rural properties in the state of Minas Gerais regarding compliance with national legislation, traceability and socio-environmental criteria for the export of agricultural commodities. The website presents information about the Minas Gerais territory, such as land use, biomes, indigenous lands, deforestation after 2008, among others. The tool establishes a certification of socio-environmental compliance, based on an integrated and automated analysis of data from the CAR system, the Continuous

[19] MAPA, AgroBrasil + Sustentável (2025).

[20] Brazil (2024).

Monitoring of Vegetation Cover by the State Institute of Forests (IEF) and high-resolution mapping of the Minas Gerais coffee park. Table 5.1 details the selected Brazilian regulations related to forests.

Brazilian regulatory framework is complemented by its implementation mechanisms. In fact, these mechanisms are responsible for the effectiveness and enforcement of norms. Table 5.2 illustrates the Brazilian forest-related mechanisms.

As observed, Brazil has a strict forest-related framework that has been developed over the last few years.[21] Yet, significant challenge consists in an effective implementation of these framework, as repeatedly discussed among Brazilian government actors.[22] Notorious example is the Casino case[23] on cattle production in the Amazon region, which has been extensively denounced for the serious environmental and human rights risks associated with the illegal occupation of public lands, loss of forest and threats to the way of life of traditional communities and indigenous peoples living in the region.

In order to delve deeper into its regulation and applicability to the EUDR, a more commodity-specific approach is required. Thus, the next section discusses the case of the coffee sector in Brazil, highlighting its functioning, mechanisms, challenges and opportunities.

5.2 A Case Study of the Coffe Sector

As mentioned previously, the coffee sector in Brazil has a leading role in its total exports to the EU. Moreover, the sector has been constantly involved in discussing the EUDR,[24] mainly regarding the industry's contributions to EUDR compliance. Therefore, a specific analysis of the sector may bring valuable lessons to other commodity supply chains. This section presents a data-driven overview of the Brazilian coffee market, reaffirming its significance in the country's international trade. It also draws on semi-structured interviews with key stakeholders to capture on-the-ground perspectives regarding the implementation of the European anti-deforestation regulation.

[21] See a summary of forest-related Brazilian regulation and mechanisms in Annex IV and V.

[22] Senado (2024).

[23] Business and Human Rights Resource Centre (2025).

[24] For instance, see: Cecafé (2024). Cecafé lança landing page sobre EUDR e os cafés do Brasil, https://www.cecafe.com.br/publicacoes/noticias/eudr-cafes-do-brasil-20240819/. Accessed 22 September 2024.; G1. (2024) Brasil está pronto para Regulamento da União Europeia para Produtos Livres de Desmatamento, https://g1.globo.com/sp/santos-regiao/especial-publicitario/seminario-internacional-do-cafe/24-seminario-internacional-do-cafe/noticia/2024/05/27/brasil-esta-pronto-para-regulamento-da-uniao-europeia-para-produtos-livres-de-desmatamento.ghtml. Accessed 23 June 2024.

Table 5.1 Selected forest-related Brazilian regulation

Regulatory Level	Diploma	Entry into force	Summary
National—Legal	**Brazilian Federal Law n. 12.651** (New Brazilian Forest Code)	25/05/2012	Addresses the preservation of native vegetation and repeals the Brazilian Forest Code of 1965, determining the responsibility of the owner of protected environments between the Permanent Preservation Area (APP) and the Legal Reserve (RL) to preserve and protect all ecosystems. The New Forest Code raises controversial points between rural and environmental interests to this day
National—Legal	**Brazilian Federal Law n. 6.938** (National Environmental Policy)	31/08/1981	Establishes the National Environmental Policy, its purposes, and mechanisms for formulation and implementation, and provides for other measures. Aims at the preservation, improvement, and recovery of environmentally beneficial quality of life, intending to ensure favorable conditions for socioeconomic development, national security interests, and protection of human life quality. Prohibits pollution, requires licensing, and regulates the appropriate use of environmental resources
National—Legal	**Brazilian Federal Law n. 9.985** (National System of Nature Conservation Units)	18/07/2000	Among its objectives are the conservation of biological species and genetic resources, the preservation and restoration of the diversity of natural ecosystems, and the promotion of sustainable development based on natural resources
National—Legal	**Brazilian Federal Law n. 6.902** (Environmental Protection Area Law)	27/04/1981	Establishes guidelines for the creation of Ecological Stations and Environmental Protection Areas (APAs). Ecological Stations are representative areas of different ecosystems in Brazil that must have 90% of their territory unchanged, and only 10% can undergo alterations for academic purposes. APAs, on the other hand, comprise private properties that can be regulated by the competent public authority regarding economic activities to protect the environment
National—Infralegal	**Normative Instruction MMA n. 2/2001**	10/05/2001	Determines that the economic exploitation of forests on rural properties located in the Legal Amazon, including areas of legal reserve and subject to permanent preservation areas established by current legislation, shall be carried out through sustainable multiple-use forest management practices

(continued)

Table 5.1 (continued)

Regulatory Level	Diploma	Entry into force	Summary
National—Infralegal	**Ordinance MMA n. 183/2001**	10/05/2001	Establishes, within the scope of the Ministry of the Environment, the Monitoring and Evaluation System for Environmental Licensing on Rural Properties in the Legal Amazon, with the aim of monitoring and evaluating licensing instruments and procedures for land use conversion, forest management, and burnings, as well as advising the Ministry of the Environment on these matters
National—Infralegal	**Normative Instruction MMA n. 2/2014**	05/05/2014	Establishes procedures for the integration, execution, and harmonization of the Rural Environmental Registry System (SICAR) and defines the general procedures for the Rural Environmental Registry (CAR)
National—Infralegal	**Ordinance MMA n. 365/2015**	21/11/2015	Establishes the Brazilian Biomes Environmental Monitoring Program with the aim of mapping and monitoring national vegetation
National—Infralegal	**Federal Decree n. 11.367/2023**	01/01/2023	Establishes the Permanent Interministerial Commission for the Prevention and Control of Deforestation, reinstates the Action Plan for the Prevention and Control of Deforestation in the Legal Amazon - PPCDAm, and outlines Action Plans for the Prevention and Control of Deforestation in the Cerrado, Atlantic Forest, Caatinga, Pampa, and Pantanal
National—Bill	**Brazilian Federal Law Project n. 3961/2020**	Not in force	Summary: Declares a state of climate emergency, establishes the goal of neutralizing greenhouse gas emissions in Brazil by 2050, and provides for the creation of policies for sustainable transition Status: Ready for Agenda in the Committee on Environment and Sustainable Development (CMADS)
National—Bill	**Brazilian Federal Law Project n. 3867/2021**	Not in force	Summary: Imposes environmental criteria for granting government subsidies to the productive chain of animal products, aiming to achieve sustainable development goals Status: Ready for Agenda in the Committee on Environment and Sustainable Development (CMADS)

(continued)

Table 5.1 (continued)

Regulatory Level	Diploma	Entry into force	Summary
National—Bill	**Brazilian Federal Law Project n. 4450/2021**	Not in force	Summary: Provides for the prohibition of registration in the Rural Environmental Registry (CAR) of rural properties in protected areas and undesignated public forests, the suspension of CAR validity on properties with illegal deforestation, and mandatory remote automatic embargo in case of illegal deforestation on rural properties, and provides for other measures Status: Transiting in Group
International	**Regulation (EU) 2018/828 of the European Parliament and of the Council** on organic production and labelling of organic products	01/01/2021	Establishes the principles of organic production and lays down the rules concerning organic production, related certification and the use of indications referring to organic production in labelling and advertising, as well as rules on controls additional to those laid down in Regulation (EU) 2017/625. It aims to revise and strengthen the European Union's (EU) rules on organic production and the labelling of organic products in relation to: the control system, the trade regime and production rules

Table 5.2 Selected Brazilian forest-related mechanisms

Supporting tools	Type	Responsable Organization	Management	Definition	Objectives	Characteristic	Link
TerraBrasilis	Instruments for measuring deforestation	National Institute for Space Research (INPE)	Federal Public	Spatial data analysis of brazilian land cover and uses	Organizing, accessing and using, through a web portal, geographic data produced by INPE	Complex algorithms; web application; interoperable; public programs database (PRODES/DETER)	https://terrabrasilis.dpi.inpe.br
Mapbiomas	Instruments for measuring deforestation	NGOs, universities and technology startups	Private	Spatial data analysis of brazilian land cover and uses	Reveals the transformations of the Brazilian territory with precision, agility and quality, and make knowledge about coverage and land use	Collaborative network; spatial data analysis; complex algorithms; web application; present throughout Latin America	https://brasil.mapbiomas.org/
Rural Environmental Registry (CAR)	Instruments for measuring deforestation	Brazilian Forest Service/Federal Government	Federal Public	National electronic public registry of all rural properties	Integrates environmental information on rural properties and possessions to control and monitor, environmental and economic planning and to combat to deforestation in Brazil	Electronic system; Federation Unit (UF) as competent state body; rural property information	https://www.car.gov.br/#/

(continued)

Table 5.2 (continued)

Supporting tools	Type	Responsable Organization	Management	Definition	Objectives	Characteristic	Link
Selo Verde Brasil (Brazil Green Seal)	Certifier	Federal Government	Federal Public	Federal public certification for all products	Develops a national strategy for certification and conformity assessment of Brazilian products and services that have proven to have a socio-environmentally responsible life cycle	Unique certification; international sustainability standards; all economy sectors included	https://www.gov.br/participamaisbrasil/programa-selo-verde-brasil
Selo Verde de Minas Gerais (Green Seal-MG)	Certifier	Government of the State of Minas Gerais Minas Gerais	State Públic	A Plataform and State public certification for agricultural commodities of MG	Highlights relevant information about the sustainability of coffee production in Minas Gerais to certify their agricultural commodities	Cooperation agreement; information about the Minas Gerais territory; sustainability of coffee production in the state; compliance with CAR and IEF	https://seloverde.meioambiente.mg.gov.br/

(continued)

Table 5.2 (continued)

Supporting tools	Type	Responsable Organization	Management	Definition	Objectives	Characteristic	Link
Brazilian Agro-Traceability System (SIBRAAR)	Tracker	Federal Government/ INMETRO	Federal Public	Federal government traceability system for agro-industrial products	Tracks agro-industrial products, offering information about their quality and origin, in a transparent and reliable way	Blockchain technology; various agricultural crops included; information about the entire production chain	https://www.embrapa.br/en/busca-de-solucoes-tecnologicas/-/produto-servico/8599/sibraar---sistema-brasileiro-de-agrorrastreabilidade

5.2.1 A Deeper Look into the Coffee Sector in Brazil

According to the International Coffee Organisation Report,[25] South America is the world's leading region in coffee production. In 2024, the continent produced 89.3 million bags of coffee, accounting for 48.3% of global production during the 2022/23 coffee year. Of this amount, 57.4% was arabica and 23.9% robusta—the two most widely consumed coffee varieties. The top producers in the region are Brazil, Colombia, and Peru, with Brazil leading in overall bean production.

Brazil is the largest producer and exporter of coffee not only in South America, but also in the world.[26] The country is responsible for around 32% of the world's exports of unroasted beans, shipping around 35.15 million bags annually. Therefore, coffee exports account for a large part of the country's revenue. Furthermore, 50% of total exports go to the EU, being Germany, Italy, Belgium, Spain and France, in that order, the biggest importers of Brazilian beans regionally.[27]

Despite its century-long history in the country, coffee production is still expanding nationally. According to data from the National Supply Company (CONAB),[28] total production in 2024, including arabica and conilon types, was estimated at 58.81 million bags, an increase of 6.8% or 3.74 million bags over the crop harvested in 2023. This data also suggests that the total area destined for coffee growing in the country in 2024, for arabica and conilon types, will total 2.25 million hectares. This means an increase of 0.5% on the area of the previous harvest, with 1.9 million hectares of crops in production and a growth of 1.5% on the previous year. On the other hand, less'traditional' sectors, such as soy industry, also face an increase of total producing area. For instance, in less than four decades, area devoted to soy grew ninefold and now accounts for 14% of all agricultural land in Brazil.[29] However, soy is largely considered one of the greatest contributors to deforestation. For instance, the sector was responsible for the loss of near 60.000 hectares between September and November 2023.[30]

In the first four months of 2024, Brazil exported 16.4 million 60-kilo bags of coffee, which corresponds to an increase of 46.5% compared to the 11.2 million bags exported in the same period in 2023. According to CONAB data, Brazil exported coffee to 124 countries in 2024. The United States and Germany were the main destinations, accounting for 17.5% and 14.4% of total export volume, respectively. They were followed by Belgium (10.5%), Italy (7.8%), and Japan (5.4%). Additionally, during the first four months of 2024, two Brazilian ports stood out in terms of shipments of Brazilian coffee abroad: the port of Santos, with 69.2% of production, and the port of Rio de Janeiro, with 22.6%, both in the country's Southeast region. The two ports together account for 91.8% of the country's coffee exports.

---

[25] ICO (2023).

[26] ICO (2024).

[27] CONAB (2014).

[28] Ibid.

[29] MapBiomas (2024).

[30] Mighty Earth (2024).

Like many agricultural sectors, coffee production may also contribute to forest and environmental degradation. Not only deforestation itself, such as the devastation of virgin forests for bean cultivation, but also several elements present in the production process can contribute to forest and environmental degradation. Moreover, the emission of greenhouse gases generated during production can affect the environment and contribute to global warming.

Brazil is the world's fourth-largest consumer of nitrogen fertilizers, receiving 95% of the imports of this resource. Globally, nitrogen fertilizers are responsible for 2% of greenhouse gas (GHG) emissions, and, in Brazil, many coffee producers continue to rely on it, which contributes to GHG emissions and increases the carbon footprint of coffee.[31] A study conducted by Cooxupé - the world's largest cooperative of coffee producers, based in Minas Gerais - and Embrapa (Brazilian Agricultural Research Corporation) found that the carbon footprint of arabica coffee in Brazil ranges from 1.9 to 4.6 kg CO_2 eq/kg coffee.[32] According to the same study, adopting 'green' fertilization practices could reduce this footprint by up to 60%..[33] As with many commodities, coffee production in Brazil still has opportunities to evolve in terms of environmental sustainability, particularly by reducing GHG emissions and by minimizing its impact on the environment.

Conversely, coffee growing is also considered an ally in building strategies to reduce the effects of global warming. According to the Cecafé[34] Project on the GHG balance of conilon coffee in Espírito Santo, coffee cultivation can be considered contributes to the reduction GHG emissions, since the crop captures carbon during the growth of the coffee tree and stores it in the biomass over an extended period..[35] Thus, there is great potential for carbon sequestration in coffee crops.

However, when considering the GHG balance of the crop's production system, there are also emissions caused by the different sources present in crop management, which involve, for example, mechanised operations, fertilisation and soil correction. As a result, the adoption of sustainable practices is becoming increasingly essential for reducing GHG emissions in agriculture. Sustainable production seeks not only to sequester an amount of carbon equivalent to what is emitted, but to go further removing more carbon from the atmosphere than it releases, thereby transforming the crop into a carbon-negative system. To achieve a negative GHG balance, it is essential to adopt practices such as the use of organic and organo-mineral fertilisers with a lower nitrogen content, solar energy, and pruning and coffee residues. In other words, to adopt good agricultural management practices.

---

[31] Brasil 2050: Rotas de Descarbonização da Economia, painel 4 (2024) Diálogos setoriais sobre opções e desafios na trajetória de descarbonização" do Seminário (22 May 2024), https://www.youtube.com/watch?v=KZyoE1IyFJ4. Accessed 25 June 2024.

[32] Forbes (2021) Pegada de carbono do café arábica vai do pé à xícara.

[33] Ibid.

[34] The association of coffee exporters in Brazil.

[35] IMAFLORA (2022) Projeto Cecafé. Balanço de Gases de Efeito Estufa do Café Conilon Capixaba, https://www.imaflora.org/public/media/biblioteca/relatorio_cecafe_imaflora.pdf. Accessed 25 June 2024.

Regarding potential EUDR compliance concerning coffee production in Brazil, few studies tried to assess potential readiness of the sector. For instance, the Institute for Sustainability (IIS) mapped the production network of six agricultural commodities in Brazil and concluded that coffee is the most likely good to comply with EUDR's requirements, while beef is the least prepared.[36] This study tried to assess the likelihood of compliance with the EUDR according to criteria such as exports, deforestation, certifications and the practice of small producers.[37]

The IIS research used the coverage of voluntary sustainability standards as one of the proxies to construct its analytical index. It was based on the assumption that sectors with prior experience in implementing environmental certifications are likely to be better prepared for compliance, having developed know-how in sustainability mechanisms and deforestation-free production practices. According to this metric, the coffee sector demonstrated the highest likelihood of compliance, with a probability of 33%.

This know-how on sustainability mechanisms and production practices in the coffee sector is related to the already existing international and national institutional initiatives. The Global Coffee Platform (GCP) is one such example. It is a multi-sectoral association dedicated to promoting sustainability in the coffee sector. The GCP enables coffee producers, traders, roasters, governments and NGOs to align their efforts, acting collectively on local priorities and critical issues, scaling up local sustainability programmes and expanding the global market for sustainable coffee throughout the coffee world.[38]

According to GCP's 2023 Annual Report, the coffee sector already has the Equivalence Mechanism (EM), which is a tool that helps stakeholders navigate the complexity of sustainability schemes in the sector. According to the platform's information, through the EM it is possible to better understand which sustainability schemes meet - at the very least - basic sustainability practices in a credible and efficient manner.

At a national level, institutions in the coffee sector already have technological-institutional apparatus capable of certifying compliance with national and international environmental standards and certifying the sustainable nature of many producers. The Minas Gerais 'Selo Verde'[39] (or 'Green Seal') is a notorious example. It is a platform developed by researchers from UFMG in partnership with the Government of Minas Gerais through the State Forestry Institute (IEF) and the Centre for Territorial Intelligence and with support from the European Union's AL-INVEST Verde programme. It provides individualised information on rural properties in Minas

[36] R. Garcia (2024) 'Café é o produto agrícola brasileiro mais próximo das novas exigências ambientais da UE. Carne é o mais distante', O Globo, https://oglobo.globo.com/um-so-planeta/noticia/2024/02/10/cafe-e-o-produto-agricola-brasileiro-mais-proximo-das-novas-exigencias-ambientais-da-ue-carne-o-e-mais-distante.ghtml. Accessed 25 June 2024.

[37] De Oliveira et al. (2024).

[38] GCP (2023).

[39] SEMAD (2024).

Gerais, mainly coffee producers, regarding compliance with national legislation, traceability and socio-environmental criteria for exporting agricultural commodities.

The website, which is the result of a co-operation agreement signed between UFMG and IEF, with the support of the Secretariat of Agriculture, Supply and Livestock (SEAPA), provides relevant information on the sustainability of coffee production in Minas Gerais. It presents information on the territory of Minas Gerais, such as land use, biomes, indigenous lands, deforestation after 2008, among others. The tool establishes a certification of socio-environmental compliance, based on an integrated and automated analysis of data from the CAR system, the Continuous Monitoring of Vegetation Cover by the State Forestry Institute (IEF) and high-resolution mapping of Minas Gerais' coffee plantations.

As another initiative, the Cecafé Seal[40] guarantees the sustainability of the coffee production chain and respect for labour and environmental laws throughout the production chain. This certificate ensures that coffee-growing areas make continuous efforts to protect water sources, adopt rational water management and apply advanced agricultural techniques to achieve significant productivity per hectare planted. It also ensures that the coffee grower adopts the same labour laws applied to urban workers on their rural property, complying with strict requirements, such as the payment of a guarantee fund, public social security, and other social benefits established by Brazilian labor law to his employees, as well as using Personal Protective Equipment when handling pesticides and having appropriate facilities for housing and feeding workers.

More recently, Cecafé developed a traceability platform, called Cafés do Brasil,[41] in order to measure and mitigate deforestation risks in its supply chain. It is a platform developed by Serasa Experian and institutionally managed by Cecafé and its members. This platform was developed from polygons and georeferenced data collected by the CAR system and vis-à-vis the Brazilian Forest Code, which aims to ensure that grain production comes from areas that have not been deforested.

5.2.2 *Interviews with Coffee Representatives*

To capture on-the-ground perception on the EUDR's implementation in Brazil, this research explores semi-structured interviews with representatives from the country's coffee sector, including producers and members of exporter and industry associations engaged with producers of varying operational scales. In the following paragraphs, interviewees are identified as 'Interviewee 1', 'Interviewee 2', 'Interviewee 3', 'Interviewee 4', and 'Interviewee 5', in the chronological order of their participation. While some discussions touched upon topics related to the international

[40] Cecafé (2024) Selo Cecafé. https://www.cecafe.com.br/sustentabilidade/selo-cecafe/. Accessed 19 Dec 2024.

[41] Cecafé (2024). Cafés do Brasil. https://www.cecafe.com.br/sustentabilidade/artigos/plataforma-de-rastreabilidade-cafes-do-brasil-20230816/. Accessed 11 Oct 2024.

scenario or to events in other countries, the primary focus remained the impacts of the EUDR implementation in Brazil - an emphasis that required deliberate efforts by the interviewers to guide the conversations on that direction.

To choose participants for this study, the authors mapped the Brazilian coffee sector to identify key stakeholders amongst producers, exporters, and associations of varying sizes. Once potential participants had been identified, the authors primarily contacted them via email, providing an overview of the research project, an invitation to participate in the interview, and a consent letter to be signed upon acceptance. As invitations were progressively accepted, the initial round of interviews was conducted. Additional participants were subsequently selected using the 'snowball sampling method', whereby previous interviewees recommended new participants for the study. Interview scripts were used to guide the conversations, allowing a degree of flexibility for both participants and interviewers and maintaining, at the same time, a careful focus on the core objective of the research, namely: to assess the impacts of the EUDR implementation in Brazil. All the interviews were conducted in Portuguese, between September 2024 and January 2025.

With assurances of confidentiality and anonymity, participants consented to the recording of their interviews, which were, then, transcribed using audio–video transcription software, and any inconsistencies in the transcripts were manually reviewed and corrected. Both audio–video files and transcription documents were stored on a private server accessible only to researchers involved in the study. Although interviewees offered different approaches and contributions, several recurring topics emerged. A word cloud of the most frequently used terms reflects such frequency, highlighting which words were used more often than others during the interviews. The most frequent words of the interviews can be seen schematically in Fig. 5.1.

As shown by the image above, the most commonly occurring word in the interviews is *café* (Portuguese for coffee).[42] The prevalence of this word confirms the importance of the sector for the country's economy and its central role for Brazilian trade relations, particularly with the European Union. In this context, analyzing the sector's perspectives and challenges offers a valuable lens through which to understand the broader implications of EUDR implementation in Brazil, especially given the coffee maket's long-standing engagement with sustainability and environmentally conscious practices.

This section is divided into two subsections. The first relates to the recurring topics frequently addressed by interviewees (b.1), while the second addresses general assessments of the interviews (b.2).

---

[42] The ten most frequent words of the interviews are: coffee (which relates to the analysed sector and its products); Brazil (concerning the territorial scope of the research); today (mostly associated with contemporary discussions); world (concerning topics related to the international scenario, such as international trade and relations); European (in reference to the EUDR and EU policies, market players and government); union (usually in reference to the European Union); inside (often used in reference to products, territory or norms); country (generically referring to countries); producer (as one of the major players concerning the EUDR implementation); and year (referring to temporally locate some phenomenon or deadline).

Fig. 5.1 Most frequent words of the interviews

5.2.2.1 Recurring Topics Frequently Addressed by Interviewees

Based in the results of the interviews, the authors also identified five recurring thematic topics frequently addressed by interviewees: Perceptions of the EUDR's Regulatory Framework (I); Brazil's Forest-Related Legal Framework (II); The Status of the Brazilian Coffee Sector in Relation to EUDR Compliance (III); Impacts on Trade (IV); and Brazilian Technologies for Certification and Monitoring (V). The main results are summarized in the table below and further analysed in the following paragraphs, where exact translations of expressions or phrases used by the interviewees appear in double quotation marks.

Perceptions of the EUDR's Regulatory Framework

The first topic, 'Perceptions of the EUDR's Regulatory Framework', captures interviewees' views on the scope, objectives, and definitional criteria of the regulation. Overall, participants expressed a positive perception of the EUDR's goals of halting deforestation and promoting sustainability. **Interviewee 1** emphasized support for the regulation's intent, stating that "We [Brazil's coffee sector] can never present ourselves to the world as being against ending deforestation. [...] We must show our numbers to prove that we're truly committed". Echoing the same position, **Interviewee 4** observed that no one—especially within the coffee sector—opposes efforts to combat deforestation, but stressed the importance of fostering broader dialogue with the European Union to ensure these efforts are carried out "in the best and most sensible way possible [...] so everyone moves forward together.". For **Interviewee 5**, producers, including coffee growers, are the most interested group in combating deforestation, since they depend upon natural resources to accesses drinking water and maintain their crops.

Still on the topic of 'perceptions regarding the EUDR's regulatory framework', **Interviewee 3** stated that the EUDR's guidelines are "correct," but acknowledged the need for adjustments and an extension of the implementation deadline. Despite the regulation's positive objectives, participants pointed out a lack of clearly defined criteria in its wording. **Interviewee 1**, for example, highlighted uncertainty about whether national regulatory frameworks—particularly the Brazilian Forestry Code, which permits a certain degree of legally authorized vegetation removal—would be accepted. He also fears that terms such as 'negligible risk'[43] lacks a proper definition and, thus, generates uncertainty. **Interviewee 2** expressed the same concern, fearing that the concept of legal deforestation, as recognized under Brazilian law, might not be acknowledged by the European regulation. According to **Interviewee 2**, many coffee-producing properties in Brazil date back to the nineteenth century and occasionally require tree removal for energy safety purposes. Those operations are typically carried out by electricity companies, not by the property owners themselves. However, it remains unclear how the EUDR will address situations like this.

Another concern raised by participants relates to the lack of consistency in the practices adopted by competent authorities. **Interviewee 5** highlighted the broad discretionary power granted to these authorities, emphasizing that the regulation's vague wording allows for costly fines to be imposed—or not—based on the subjective interpretation or disposition of officials. He also warned that strict enforcement could lead to supply shortages, while overly lenient implementation risks compromising the EU's credibility. **Interviewee 1**, in turn, pointed to the lack of standardized procedures across ports, except for Hamburg, Antwerp, and Rotterdam, which have signed a cooperation agreement.

In sum, while all interviewees expressed strong support for the EUDR's overarching goals of halting deforestation and fostering sustainability, their perceptions of the regulation's framework reveal important concerns regarding its clarity, consistency, and implementation. Participants emphasized the need for well-defined criteria, greater alignment with national laws such as the Brazilian Forestry Code, and more predictable and harmonized implementation practices across competent authorities and ports. Without these improvements, they warn that the regulation

[43] EURD's Article 2 (26) briefly describes it as'the level of risk that applies to relevant commodities and relevant products, where, on the basis of a full assessment of product-specific and general information, and, where necessary, of the application of the appropriate mitigation measures, those commodities or products show no cause for concern as being not in compliance with Article 3, point (a) or (b)'. For instance, criteria or requirements should be further expanded in order to provide a practical definition.

could inadvertently generate uncertainty, hinder trade, and weaken its own credibility, despite its positive intent.

Brazil's Forest-Related Legal Framework

Regarding the topic 'Brazil's Forest-Related Legal Framework', participants acknowledge that Brazil possesses a well-developed legal framework for forest management, particularly centred on the Forestry Code. **Interviewee 2** stated that Brazilian forest related legislation "[...] is not the kind of legislation that causes any discomfort or problems [for the coffee sector]. In my view, it meets what we consider important and necessary". According to **Interviewee 1**, the country's legal framework is responsible for providing an environment of legality in the national agribusiness sector, with a high degree of data-collection and transparency. This level of legality is highly maintained by formal procedures within the economic and commercial practices, especially with the nationwide implementation of the electronic invoicing system.

As observed by **Interviewee 3**, the country's average coffee productivity used to be around 7 to 8 bags per hectare, whereas today the national average—considering both arabica and robusta types—has reached 34 bags. Hence, over the past 34 years, production has more than quadrupled while the planted area has decreased by 10%, which **Interviewee 3** sees as a clear demonstration of sustainability being deeply rooted in the country's agricultural practices. Despite this statement, as demonstrated in the section above, CONAB has recorded a 0.5% increase on coffee's cultivated area in 2024, compared with the previous harvest-year.

Regarding 'Brazil's Forest-Related Legal Framework', participants expressed a consistent view that Brazil's legal framework is both robust and conducive to sustainable agricultural practices. Anchored by the Forestry Code, the legislation is perceived not as a burden but as a necessary foundation that supports legal compliance and sectoral stability. The integration of formal procedures—such as electronic invoicing—further reinforces transparency and accountability within agribusiness. Moreover, the significant increase in coffee productivity underscores how legal compliance and sustainability have advanced, reflecting a broader commitment to responsible land use in Brazil's coffee sector.

The Status of the Brazilian Coffee Sector in Relation to EUDR Compliance

Under the topic 'The Status of the Brazilian Coffee Sector in Relation to EUDR Compliance', interviewees generally agreed that, among the various sectors and countries impacted by the European regulation, Brazil's coffee sector stands out as one of the most prepared to meet its demands. **Interviewee 2**, for instance, does not view the EUDR provisions as a surprise, but rather as an opportunity for Brazilian exporters to expand their consumer base. She emphasized that the country's coffee producers typically follow sustainable practices, including what she described as "regenerative agriculture, which is about passing on to future generations a soil that is better than the one existing today."

Similarly, **Interviewee 1** described Brazilian coffee as a "friendly commodity," highlighting its positive reputation among European importers. He also noted that Brazil's coffee plantations are more established than those of other crops, which, in his view, increases their capacity to comply with the EUDR. **Interviewee 3** echoed this perspective, stating that the coffee sector as a whole—including producers, exporters, industry representatives, and consumers—has maintained a decade-long commitment to sustainability.

Interviewee 2, while maintaining her position about the overall readiness of the sector, expressed concerns about the regulation's applicability to small and medium-sized exporters, whose operations are often family-run and relatively informal. In the same sense, **Interviewee 4** emphasized not only the costs of complying with the EUDR but also the burden of proving such compliance to the EU—factors that may pose significant challenges for smaller exporters. **Interviewee 5** added that, although small and medium-sized coffee producers can benefit from the support of cooperatives, many still engage in informal practices, such as selling without issuing invoices or underreporting transaction values, to—among other reasons- remain eligible for government minimum income assistance.

In sum, the Brazilian coffee sector is widely regarded by interviewees as well-positioned to comply with the EUDR—thanks to its longstanding sustainability practices, positive international reputation, and established production systems. However, concerns remain about the uneven capacity to meet some of the norm's requirements across different scales of operation. Small and medium-sized exporters may face significant barriers related to informality, limited resources, and the high costs of demonstrating compliance.

Impacts on Trade

The topic 'Impacts on Trade' also reflects concerns about the potentially unequal burden that EUDR adaptation costs may place on small and medium-sized producers, as well as the broader implications the regulation may have on commercial transactions. **Interviewee 5** stated that, to export to EU, "smaller producers will have to start issuing formal invoices, and this will create a new market dynamic", which is still not predictable. **Interviewee 2** anticipates increased market concentration in favour of larger exporters, as smaller producers are being pushed to join bigger exporter associations. She also noted that even large-scale producers are experiencing a decline in sales due to uncertainties surrounding the implementation of the EUDR. In this scenario, importers are concerned about potential fines and are requesting that producers (at their own expense) store coffee bags for later importation. Similarly, **Interviewee 5** reported having witnessed deals fall through due to importers' doubts about exporters' compliance with the EUDR, stating that even the slightest uncertainty can lead to delays in closing deals or outright cancellations.

Interviewee 5 also mentioned concerns on logistics challenges and shipment delays, since shipments that used to take around 28 to 42 days could take up to 150 days to reach destinations in Europe, due to the requirements of EUDR. Additionally, with the EUDR's digital systems still unavailable or uncertain, exporters are hesitant to ship their production, since, if a shipment is already at sea when the regulation begins, it could face serious compliance risks. According to **Interviewee 5**, as a result, many traders might delay exports until they understand how enforcement will actually work—raising the risk of supply shortages in Europe.

Participants foresee potential impacts of EUDR implementation on trade and significant challenges on this regard, particularly for small and medium-sized producers. These challenges include the increased administrative and logistic costs, market concentration favouring larger exporters, and disruptions in commercial transactions due to compliance uncertainties. Furthermore, logistical issues, such as extended shipment delays, exacerbate the situation, while the absence of a clear digital system for compliance adds to the uncertainty.

Brazilian Technologies for Certification and Monitoring

On the topic 'Brazilian Technologies for Certification and Monitoring', participants identified potential incompatibility between the country's systems and the criteria adopted by the EU. **Interviewee 4**, for instance, stated that coffee and cocoa have become "scapegoats" of the EUDR, as they were not initially meant to be included in the deforestation regulation. However, due to the influence of major certifiers, these commodities—among the most certified in the world—were added to the list of regulated products. The rationale was that they could serve as positive examples for more environmentally harmful commodities, such as cattle, soy, and palm oil, whose production is considered less sustainable. Nevertheless, **Interviewee 1** highlighted that these certifiers tend to undermine the complexity of EUDR's requirements and have engaged in political misunderstandings with coffee exporters.

In this scenario, according to **Interviewee 3**, Brazil has started to adapt its certification, traceability and monitoring technologies to meet international criteria and "to get the coffee into the European Union". He argued that the systems available in the country need to accord with European requirement, since EU is a major coffee client, and Brazil should "prove sustainable practices through numbers". In other words, **Interviewee 3** sees Brazilian certification methods as internally effective, but thinks they still need to adapt to external markets, which could contribute to add value to the Brazilian coffee. Similarly, **Interviewee 2** considers the certification systems available in Brazil less effective than the international ones and fears that inconsistencies in mapping neighbouring properties could generate unfair obstacles to the exports of fully complying producers. In contrast, she also praised the 'Certifica Minas' as one of the most precise certification systems, being more meticulous than non-Brazilian alternatives, since its developers know the country's particularities.

The CAR was frequently mentioned by participants; and, while some praised the mechanism, many also cited challenges in its operation process. **Interviewee 3** sees CAR system as a positive tool for deforestation monitoring but emphasised the need for adaptation to the EUDR criteria and for provision of more accurate data. **Interviewee 4**, in turn, noted that CAR was initially regarded as Brazil's solution for complying with the European regulation. However, she cautioned that CAR may provide more information than what EUDR actually requires, since it maps entire properties, while the European regulation only mandates monitoring of areas where coffee is cultivated. According to **Interviewee 4**, this could potentially increase European oversight of Brazilian territory, so, by using CAR to meet EUDR compliance, landowners might end up "creating a trap for themselves". **Interviewee 5** expressed a similar concern, adding that Brazilian law permits a certain level of deforestation, but the European regulation follows a zero-tolerance approach. As a result, using CAR in this context could create risky situations for Brazilian producers.

Interviewee 2 also expressed concerns about using CAR as a Brazilian solution for EUDR compliance. She noted that, although the system could serve as a "first layer of safety" for the country, its data relies entirely on self-declarations by landholders, without any government verification. As a result, since property boundaries are defined by the landholders themselves, the CAR system contains numerous overlapping property claims, which leads to deforestation false positives. **Interviewee 1** also raised concerns about potential false positives stemming from CAR data. However, within the coffee sector, he views these as "minor issues" that could likely be resolved through open dialogue with European authorities.

Brazilian technologies for certification, traceability, and monitoring were recognized by participants as advanced and promising, yet not fully aligned with the criteria established by the EUDR. While tools such as the CAR and initiatives like Certifica Minas were praised for their scope and precision, concerns persist regarding data reliability, lack of government verification, and potential mismatches with European requirements. These challenges are especially critical when systems originally designed for national purposes are expected to meet external regulatory demands.

5.2.2.2 General Assessment of the Interviews

The main results of the interviews, described on the previous section, are summarised in Table 5.3.

Overall, interviewees expressed strong support for the EUDR's core goals of halting deforestation and promoting sustainability, highlighting Brazil's robust legal framework and the coffee sector's long-standing commitment to responsible production. However, they also underscored key implementation challenges, including regulatory ambiguities, discrepancies in implementation, and disproportionate impacts on small and medium-sized exporters. Concerns about trade disruptions, compliance costs, and logistical uncertainties further complicate the scenario. Moving forward, participants emphasized the need for clearer regulatory criteria, closer alignment between national and international standards, and open dialogue between Brazilian stakeholders and European authorities. Such efforts are essential to ensure that the

Table 5.3 Interview's main topics

Topic	Description
Perceptions of the EUDR's Regulatory Framework	Participants consider the scope/objective of the EUDR (deforestation mitigation) to be valid and support policy efforts on this matter. However, they believe that the EUDR surpass EU's competence and is poorly drafted, thus bringing negative impacts globally. They also identify a lack of clarity about EUDR's criteria, specially concerning due diligence requirements and the recognition of third country mechanisms
Brazil's Forest-Related Legal Framework	Participants recognise that Brazil has an advanced forest-related framework. However, some criticised its effective implementation
The Status of the Brazilian Coffee Sector in Relation to EUDR Compliance	In general, the coffee sector in Brazil is considered well-advanced and one of the lowest contributors to deforestation
Impacts on Trade	There are already impacts on trade, mostly due to doubts concerning the application of the EUDR. Additionally, there is an expectation that costs of adaptation may burden mainly small and medium-sized producers (SMEs)
Brazilian Technologies for Certification and Monitoring	Unclear EUDR criteria and differing methodologies may create incompatibilities between Brazil's systems and the EU's requirements. While Brazil's technologies and certifications are well established domestically, they require methodological adaptations to meet EU standards. Additionally, the EUDR is triggering competition among certifiers, potentially burdening producers Specifically, the CAR system faces two key issues: its self-declaratory nature limits monitoring, and its property-based structure may conflict with EUDR land plot requirements

EUDR not only achieves its environmental objectives but also supports fair and inclusive participation from all segments of Brazil's coffee sector.

5.3 Assessing Challenges from the Coffee Sector Experience

By combining an analysis of the Brazilian legal framework, data from the coffee sector, and insights from the interviews, several challenges emerged regarding the indirect implementation of the EUDR in Brazil. These challenges can be grouped into three main categories: (a) Normative Definitions; (b) Due Diligence; (c) Disproportionate Impacts of EUDR Implementation on SMEs.

5.3.1 Normative Definitions

Participants have highlighted the need for the EU to sharpen several key EUDR definitions—most notably "deforestation," "negligible risk," and "plot of land." The current regulatory text does not provide precise definitions of these terms, thus allowing for divergent interpretations. As a result, domestic definitions used in Brazil and other third countries may clash with the EUDR's intent, underscoring the need for closer dialogue with EU stakeholders to harmonize terminologies.

Even where definitions exist, they can still be conceptually incomplete. For instance, the EUDR adopts FAO's forest definition, which has limited global acceptance. Additionally, some countries, such as Brasil, do not use a single forest definition, due to its ecological diversity, exceeding FAO's and EUDR's framework.

The 2024 Guidance made progress in addressing some of these ambiguities, yet many practical details remain undefined. Full clarity will likely depend on the operationalization of competent authorities.[44] Each authority may develop its own interpretative guidelines and administrative requirements, thereby complicating due diligence processes. The wide range of institutions designated as competent authorities only amplifies this risk of inconsistent application.[45]

To achieve a coherent and enforceable EUDR regime, the legislative text must incorporate explicit, minimum criteria for all competent authorities and draw on established definitions from multilateral instruments. This dual approach will help ensure both legal certainty and broader international alignment.

5.3.2 Due Diligence

The EUDR's due diligence requirements are both extensive and complex. EU operators and traders must complete a series of steps to comply with the regulation, including engaging stakeholders throughout their supply chains. Exporters and producers from third countries—including Brazil—must not only comply with domestic legislation but also generate comprehensive information about their operations. This demands mechanisms for monitoring, certification, and traceability that are compatible with the EUDR framework.

A major challenge, however, stems from the regulation's lack of clear criteria and guidance on how competent authorities will apply the EUDR in practice. This gap creates uncertainty, as these authorities may not fully consider the specific characteristics of national mechanisms. Although Brazil's coffee sector is often regarded as "ready" to meet EUDR requirements, the regulation and its supporting documents do not provide a comprehensive methodology to assess whether operations are deforestation-free, compliant with domestic laws, and fully aligned with due

[44] As mentioned before, until the end of 2024 not all EU member countries had appointed their respective authorities.

[45] E.g. police, environmental and food-related departments.

diligence obligations. This creates a level of risk concerning the EU's potential acceptance of Brazilian systems.

Technological capacity also plays a critical role in meeting due diligence obligations. Brazilian satellite and monitoring tools must ensure that their data complies with both national and EU standards. While interviewees recognized the country's technologies as advanced and promising, they also highlighted gaps in alignment with EUDR criteria. The CAR system, in particular, drew criticism for its reliance on self-declared data by landholders, which undermines its accuracy and reliability.

Additional concerns relate to the EUDR's Information System (IS), particularly regarding how it will handle submitted data. Stakeholders questioned whether current technologies can meet its requirements. For instance, the 25 MB file size limit may be too restrictive for satellite imagery, which typically exceeds this size. Likewise, the system's exclusive reliance on the GeoJSON format may limit compatibility with other technological platforms. Adapting to the IS may require investments in training and system upgrades—costs that large companies can likely absorb but which could place significant strain on small and medium exporters (SMEs), both technically and financially.

5.3.3 Disproportionate Impacts of EUDR Implementation on SMEs

The European regulation gives insufficient consideration to the most vulnerable groups of commodity producers, particularly small and medium-sized exporters (SMEs). SMEs face heightened risks of experiencing disproportionate negative impacts from the EUDR's implementation, especially in the form of trade disruptions and high adaptation costs. While the coffee sector as a whole shows signs of preparedness for the EUDR, the regulation presents significant challenges for this group of exporters, whose businesses are often family-run and operate with relatively informal structures, making EUDR compliance demanding and costly. Beyond the financial burden of adapting to new requirements, SMEs also face the complex task of proving compliance—an obligation that could hinder their competitiveness in the EU market.

In this scenario, a key issue is the persistence of informal practices among small and medium-sized producers. Despite occasional support from cooperatives, many of them continue to sell products without issuing formal invoices or to underreport transaction values. These behaviors are not merely the result of informality but often reflect strategic decisions—such as maintaining eligibility for government income support programs. As a result, the implementation of the EUDR is expected to disproportionately affect these producers, not only due to the financial burden of compliance, but also because of the structural changes required. Formalizing business practices—such as adopting consistent invoicing procedures and implementing traceability protocols—may demand significant operational restructuring, disrupting long-standing commercial routines and introducing greater uncertainty into trade relationships.

Disproportionate challenges faced by SMEs under the EUDR could accelerate market concentration, as smaller exporters may be forced to join larger cooperatives or align with major trading firms to meet the regulation's demands. Notably, even large-scale producers are experiencing disruptions, including a decline in exports driven by growing hesitation among EU buyers. This climate of uncertainty is already impacting trade dynamics, with delays or cancellation in negotiations due to concerns about exporters' ability to meet EUDR requirements. Even minor doubts around compliance have proven enough to stall transactions, underscoring the urgent need for clearer guidance and more consistent enforcement mechanisms to ensure legal certainty and market stability. Thus, potential litigation could arise due to contractual implications.

5.4 Section Conclusion

Brazil has developed a complex and multi-layered forest governance framework that reflects both the challenges and opportunities of managing vast and diverse ecosystems. Over time, the country has transitioned from fragmented and sectoral regulations to a comprehensive legal and institutional system, encompassing robust constitutional protections, detailed environmental legislation, and increasingly sophisticated monitoring and traceability tools. Innovations such as the Rural Environmental Registry (CAR), SINAFLOR, and TerraBrasilis demonstrate Brazil's growing capacity to track and manage land use. Meanwhile, programs like PPCDAM and the National REDD+ Strategy reflect the country's commitment to aligning forest governance with climate action and sustainable development goals.

Despite notable progress, the effectiveness of Brazil's forest-related policies continues to rely heavily on political will, inter-agency coordination, and public participation. Challenges remain in ensuring compliance, addressing illegal deforestation, and strengthening enforcement mechanisms. Nonetheless, the renewed efforts under recent administrations, the revitalization of monitoring platforms, and the introduction of sustainability-oriented certification programs like the Brazil Green Seal signal a promising trajectory. If properly implemented and supported, these measures may not only reinforce Brazil's role as a key player in global forest conservation but also enhance the socio-environmental sustainability of its agribusiness sector.

Within this broader environmental governance landscape, Brazil's coffee sector plays a critical role both in the global market and in the national economy, showing strong performance in production, exportation, and sustainability advancements. Despite ongoing environmental challenges such as deforestation and GHG emissions, the sector has demonstrated significant potential for compliance with evolving sustainability standards like the European Union Deforestation Regulation (EUDR).

The interviews with representatives from Brazil's coffee sector, conducted by this study, reveal a complex but largely forward-looking stance toward the EUDR. While there is widespread support for the regulation's environmental goals, concerns emerge around its operational clarity, compatibility with Brazil's legal and technological frameworks, and the uneven effects it may have on producers of different scales. The coffee sector in Brazil appears well-positioned in terms of sustainability practices and institutional readiness, yet the successful implementation of the EUDR will depend on resolving gaps in regulatory definitions, adapting domestic monitoring systems, and ensuring equitable conditions for small and medium-sized producers. Strengthening dialogue between Brazil and the EU and fostering mutual recognition of systems and practices are vital steps in ensuring that regulatory compliance advances both environmental integrity and trade fairness.

These insights from the coffee sector illustrate that the indirect implementation of the EUDR in Brazil presents challenges that extend beyond the sector itself. Ambiguities in key definitions, operational hurdles in due diligence, structural vulnerabilities of SMEs, and misalignments with the international trade regime all contribute to an ambiance of legal uncertainty and market hesitation. While Brazil has demonstrated willingness and technological capacity to adapt, significant gaps remain between domestic mechanisms and EUDR expectations. Without clearer guidance, harmonized standards, and targeted support—particularly for small and medium exporters—the regulation risks reinforcing inequalities within the supply chain and disrupting long-established trade flows. Addressing these challenges through constructive international cooperation will be essential to unlock the full potential of sustainable trade between Brazil and the European Union.

References

Brasil 2050: Rotas de Descarbonização da Economia, painel 4 (2024) Diálogos setoriais sobre opções e desafios na trajetória de descarbonização" do Seminário (22 May 2024) https://www.youtube.com/watch?v=KZyoE1IyFJ4. Accessed 25 June 2024

Brazil. Law 6938/1981 (1981)

Brazil. Cadastro Ambiental Rural (2024)

Brazil. Complementary Law 140/2011 (2011)

Brazil. Decree 11.548/2023 (2024)

Brazil. Decree 23.793/1934 (1934)

Brazil. Decree No. 12.063/2024 (2024).

Brazil. Law 11.284/2006 (2006)

Brazil. Law 12.651/2012 Brazilian Forest Code

Brazil. Law 4771/1965 (1965)

Brazil. Federal Decree No. 73.030/1973 (1973)

Brazil. Law 9.985/2000 (2000)

Brazil. SISNAMA (2024)

Brazil. Federal Constitution (1988)

Brazil (2023) Ministério do Meio Ambiente e Mudança do Clima (MMA), Plano de Ação para Prevenção e Controle do Desmatamento na Amazônia Legal https://www.gov.br/mma/pt-br/assuntos/combate-aodesmatamento/amazonia-ppcdam-1. Accessed 22 June 2024

Brazilian Institute of the Environment and Renewable Natural Resources (2024) SINAFLOR—The national system for controlling the origin of forest products. https://www.gov.br/ibama/pt-br/servicos/sistemas/sinaflor. Accessed 22 June 2024

Business and Human Rights Resource Centre (2025) Relatório "Caso Casino: A Ligação entre o abastecimento de carne do Grupo Casino, desmatamento e violações de direitos dos povos que habitam a Terra Indígena Uru-Eu-Wau-Wau na Amazônia brasileira". https://www.business-humanrights.org/pt/latest-news/report-casino-case-the-connections-between-the-casinos-group-meet-supply-deforestation-and-violations-of-the-rights-of-the-peoples-inhabiting-the-uru-eu-wau-wau-indigenous-land-in-the-brazilian-amazon/. 22 April 2024

Cecafé (2024) Selo Cecafé. https://www.cecafe.com.br/sustentabilidade/selo-cecafe/. Accessed 19 December 2024

CONAB (2014) Acompanhamento da safra brasileira de café 1 (1). CONAB, Brasília. https://www.conab.gov.br/info-agro/safras/cafe/boletim-da-safra-de-cafe/item/download/1175_49bef97f7bf48acab4ed03bec0df47. Accessed 28 July 2024

Conselho Nacional de Justiça. Protocolo para Julgamento de Ações Ambientais (2023)

de Oliveira S, et al (2024) The European Union and United Kingdom's deforestation-free supply chains regulations: Implications for Brazil. Ecological Economics, 217

Forbes (2021) Pegada de carbono do café arábica vai do pé à xícara. https://forbes.com.br/forbesagro/2021/12/pegada-de-carbono-do-cafe-arabica-vai-do-pe-a-xicara/. Accessed 22 June 2024

Garcia R (2024) Café é o produto agrícola brasileiro mais próximo das novas exigências ambientais da UE. Carne é o mais distante. O Globo https://oglobo.globo.com/um-so-planeta/noticia/2024/02/10/cafe-e-o-produto-agricola-brasileiro-mais-proximo-das-novas-exigencias-ambientais-da-ue-carne-o-e-mais-distante.ghtml. Accessed 25 June 2024

GCP (2023) Annual Report 2023. https://www.globalcoffeeplatform.org/latest/2024/gcp-annual-report-2023/. Accessed 25 June 2024

ICO (2024) Exports of all forms of coffee by exporting countries to all destinations. https://ico.org/prices/m1-exports.pdf. accessed 25 June 2024

ICO (2023) Coffee report and outlook. https://icocoffee.org/documents/cy2023-24/Coffee_Report_and_Outlook_December_2023_ICO.pdf. Accessed 22 July 2024

IMAFLORA (2022) Projeto Cecafé. Balanço de Gases de Efeito Estufa do Café Conilon Capixaba https://www.imaflora.org/public/media/biblioteca/relatorio_cecafe_imaflora.pdf. Accessed 25 June 2024

MapBiomas (2024) Pastagem, soja e cana ocupam 77% da área de agropecuária no Brasil. https://brasil.mapbiomas.org/2024/12/06/pastagem-soja-e-cana-ocupam-77-da-area-de-agropecuaria-no-brasil/. Accessed 10 January 2025

MMA (2024) CONAMA. https://conama.mma.gov.br/. Accessed 22 December 2024

Moura A (2016) Trajetória da política ambiental federal no Brasil. https://repositorio.ipea.gov.br/handle/11058/8470. Accessed 22 June 2024

Mighty Earth (2024) Monitorando o desmatamento nas cadeias de commodities brasileiras. chrome-extension://efaidnbmnnnibpcajpcglclefindmkaj/https://mightyearth.org/wp-content/uploads/2024/11/Mighty-Earth-_Rapid-Response-Soy-Report-2-March-2024_Portuguese.pdf. accessed 10 Jan 2025

SEMAD (2024) SeloVerde MG. https://seloverde.meioambiente.mg.gov.br/. Accessed 17 Oct 2024

Senado (2024) Debate mostra que implementação do Código Florestal e do CAR ainda é desafio. https://www12.senado.leg.br/noticias/materias/2024/06/20/debate-mostra-que-implementacao-do-codigo-florestal-e-do-car-ainda-e-desafio. Accessed 20 Nov 2024

Chapter 6
General Conclusion

This book analysed the normative and regulatory challenges of the EUDR's indirect implementation in Brazil. Particularly, it aimed to answer the following research question: what are the normative and regulatory challenges policymakers and economic players face when indirectly implementing the EUDR in Brazil? In order to answer this research question, the authors discussed (a) the key justifications for the European Union's unilateral approach, exemplified by trade-related environmental measures like the EUDR, in addressing global deforestation, and the *Brussels Effect*'s contribution to the potential global impact of such measures; (b) the key challenges and potential areas of incompatibility within Brazil's existing normative and regulatory framework concerning deforestation and forest degradation that may influence the indirect implementation of the EUDR; (c) mechanisms to resolve potential conflicts arising from the implementation of the EUDR, as well as scenarios and possible solutions; and (d) the impact of the EUDR in Brazil through the perception of key stakeholders in the coffee sector regarding the challenges and opportunities associated with the indirect implementation of the European norm.

Through legislation, data and empirical analysis, this book demonstrated Brazil's willingness and technological capacity to adapt to the EUDR. Yet significant gaps remain between domestic mechanisms and the norm's requirements. Without clearer guidance, harmonized standards, and targeted support—thus persisting the challenges identified in this research—the EUDR may reinforce inequalities within the supply chain and disrupt long-established trade flows. Brazilian stakeholders, on their part, may focus on enhancing implementation mechanisms, as well as fostering open dialogues with EU counterparts in order to develop common grounds for the norm's implementation. A two-sided approach thus is required to guarantee a 'smooth' implementation of the EUDR in Brazil.

This research has faced some shortcomings. One of its limitations stems from the fact that the EUDR is not yet fully in force. This temporal aspect presents a methodological challenge, as it requires a degree of forecasting the regulation's future impacts. This challenge is further complemented by the relative lack of detailed

P. Wojcikiewicz Almeida et al., *The Normative and Regulatory Challenges for the Implementation of the European Deforestation-Free Regulation in Third Affected Countries*, https://doi.org/10.1007/978-3-032-08458-3_6

guidance and comprehensive supporting documentation from the EU, which would ideally provide greater clarity and specificity for analysis. Consequently, the research is compelled to engage in a certain amount of predictive analysis to anticipate the potential ramifications and long-term effects of the EUDR, introducing an element of uncertainty into the assessment.

Moreover, the interviews of the study were restricted to Brazilian coffee sector's stakeholders and aimed to understand not only the theoretical challenges associated with the EUDR in Brazil, but also its impacts as perceived by actors on the ground. Overall, interviewees highlighted both the sector's level of preparedness to meet the regulation's requirements and the practical obstacles hindering smoother implementation. Some findings—such as ambiguities in the regulatory text and mismatches between Brazilian and European verification systems—may be relevant to different sectors covered by the EUDR. However, other results, particularly the perceived sector's status to comply with the regulation, appear specific to the coffee market and should not be generalised.

Conducting interview-based research depends heavily on the availability and willingness of respondents to participate. Even though the interviewees featured in this book represent a diverse set of stakeholders within the sector under analysis, many were recruited using the 'snowball sampling method', where initial participants referred others to take part in the research. While this approach is effective in laying the groundwork for dialogue, it may also impose limitations to the research's scope. Notably, this study was unable to include small and medium-sized exporters—a significant shortcoming, given that several interviewees emphasized potential consequences of the EUDR implementation on SMEs, such as the exacerbation of market disparities.

Not only is the availability of participants crucial for conducting the study, but so is the access to official data. In this regard, the research encountered challenges in obtaining information from the European Union. For example, meetings of the Multi-Stakeholder Platform and of the EUDR Committee are not open to the public. While their final meeting minutes are usually made available, the detailed scope of their discussions remains inaccessible.

To overcome the constraints identified in this study, future research could take some actions. First, expanding the participant pool by including stakeholders from other sectors covered by the EUDR would provide a fuller understanding of the regulation's impact across various commodity markets in Brazil and\or other impacted countries. Second, increasing collaboration with a broader range of actors, namely medium and small-scale producers, would ensure that the unique challenges and contributions of all groups are considered. Additionally, improving access to official data from the European Union may be achieved by pushing for greater transparency in regulatory discussions. This could involve requesting wider access to meeting records or directly engaging with EU bodies to make important information available to researchers and stakeholders. Finally, efforts should be made to clarify any ambiguities in the regulatory framework and resolve mismatches between Brazilian and European verification systems, which could lead to smoother implementation of the EUDR and to a non-contentious scenario.

MIX
Papier aus verantwortungsvollen Quellen
Paper from responsible sources
FSC® C105338

If you have any concerns about our products,
you can contact us on
ProductSafety@springernature.com

In case Publisher is established outside the EU,
the EU authorized representative is:
Springer Nature Customer Service Center GmbH
Europaplatz 3, 69115 Heidelberg, Germany

Printed by Libri Plureos GmbH
in Hamburg, Germany